The First Discourse of the Buddha

THE FIRST DISCOURSE OF THE BUDDHA

Turning • The • Wheel • Of • Dhamma

Venerable Dr. Rewata Dhamma

Foreword by Venerable Ajahn Sumedho

Wisdom Publications • Boston

WISDOM PUBLICATIONS
199 Elm Street
Somerville, Massachusetts 02144

Library of Congress Cataloging-in-Publication Data
Rewatadhamma, Bhadanta.
The First Discourse of the Buddha: Turning the wheel of Dhamma / Rewata Dhamma ; foreword by Ajahn Sumedho.
p. cm.
ISBN 0-86171-104-1 (alk. paper)
1. Tipiṭaka. Suttapiṭaka. Saṃyuttanikāya. Dhammacakkapavattana Sutta—Criticism, interpretation, etc. I. Tipiṭaka. Suttapiṭaka. Saṃyuttanikāya. Dhammacakkapavattana Sutta. English.
BQ1339.5.D457R48 1997
294.3'823—DC20 96–9912

ISBN 0-8617-104-1

03 02 01 00 99
7 6 5 4 3

Cover Art: Bas-relief carving depicting the Buddha's encounter with a rice cutter taken from the great 9th century Javanese stupa of Borobudur, Indonesia.

Designed by: L·J·SAWLIT

Wisdom Publications' books are printed on acid-free paper and meet the guidelines for the permanence and durability of the Committee on Production Guidelines for Book Longevity of the Council on Library Resources.

Printed in the United States of America.

Contents

Foreword

THIS EXCELLENT TRANSLATION and comprehensive exposition of the *Dhammacakkappavattana Sutta* emphasizes the importance of practice for realizing the Four Noble Truths. This sutta is the essential teaching of the Lord Buddha leading to complete enlightenment. Yet this most profound and fundamental discourse is oftentimes overlooked in favor of the commentarial works on teachings that came later.

The truth of the matter is that this first sermon is perfect in itself. By this I mean that, if you had nothing else but this sermon to follow, it would give you all the necessary information and instruction for profound insight into the truth of what "is"—which is, of course, enlightenment.

I have used this sutta as my main guide to practice over the past twenty-eight years, constantly referring to and reflecting upon the Four Noble Truths, the three aspects of each truth, and the twelve insights—even memorizing the Pāli form for chanting.

The Buddha established his teaching on the universal truth of the impermanence of the conditioned world. This quality of impermanence is the focus for meditation and contemplation so that the grasping tendencies of our conditioned attitudes and assumptions may be recognized and relinquished, leaving the mind free of its conditioned habits. This allows for perfect knowledge and insight to arise.

The Venerable Dr. Rewata Dhamma is able to speak from scholarly and meditative experience. Therefore, this work is most significant and very much needed. Most of the Pāli Canon has been translated by scholars who, though accurate in translation, do not have insight into Buddhadhamma through the practice of vipassanā meditation. The Venerable Rewata Dhamma has made his knowledge available in this important translation and commentary.

I offer my appreciation and gratitude to the Venerable Dr. Rewata Dhamma for writing this superb work.

Ajahn Sumedho
(Phra Sumedhachariya)
Amaravati Buddhist Monastery
Great Gaddesdon, Hertfordshire, England

Preface

Two months after the Buddha attained enlightenment, he delivered his first discourse to five ascetics in Deer Park near Varanasi. This first discourse has come to be known as the *Dhammacakkappavattana Sutta*, which means the "discourse on the turning of the wheel of Dhamma." Popularly, it is known simply as the *Dhammacakka Sutta* (the *Wheel of Dhamma Discourse*). This sutta represents the essence of the Buddha's teachings. All of his subsequent teachings over the remaining forty-five years of his life were more or less based on it. In this first discourse, the Buddha explained the way to freedom from universal suffering through the teachings of the Four Noble Truths and the Noble Eightfold Middle Path free from the extremes of self-mortification and self-indulgence.

In Burma and in other Theravādin countries, Buddhists learn the *Dhammacakka Sutta* by heart and recite it daily. On special occasions, such as festivals or full-moon days, special groups or associations meet to chant the sutta in unison. Yet, despite this devotion to the recitation of the sutta, many Buddhists merely recite the *Dhammacakka Sutta* out of devotion without understanding its full meaning and practical import. Though the sutta concerns meditation directly, translations in Burmese, English, and other languages typically give only the literal meaning of this important discourse. Rarely are its practical implications elaborated. One great exception is the nine expositions on the sutta by the late Mahasi Sayadaw of Burma. Mahasi Sayadaw is renowned as the greatest vipassanā meditation master of this century. His exposition of the *Dhammacakka Sutta* elucidates for Buddhist meditation practitioners the precise steps required for the realization of the Dhamma. Mahasi's expositions were originally presented in the Burmese vernacular for a lay Burmese audience and were then translated into English by U Ko Lay, the retired rector of Mandalay University.

Most of the books available on Theravāda Buddhism in English explain the Four Noble Truths and the Noble Eightfold Path. It is rare, however, to find any writings that present the practical aspects and experiences of the meditator.

In this book I aim to further explicate the practical aspects of the sutta by drawing on the work of Mahasi Sayadaw and elaborating on the sutta in detail according to the Burmese monastic scholarly tradition and my own experience. While I was in India in the 1960s, I made a Hindi translation from the Burmese of the *Dhammacakka Sutta* based on the commentary of the Honorable U Nu, former prime minister of Burma. U Nu was ordained as a monk at Mahasi Meditation Center in Rangoon after being freed from house arrest in the late 1960s. He taught on the *Dhammacakka Sutta* on several occasions in Burma before he went to India in 1969. That book, while it covered the same material as this one, was based on a one-and-a-half-hour-long oral presentation of the text that was given to a mainstream Burmese audience. This new English edition explains each paragraph of the original sutta in greater detail and, while directed primarily at the meditation practitioner, is also useful to individuals interested in the essential teachings of Buddhism, the historical life of the Buddha, the philosophical, historical, and religious background at the time of the Buddha as well as in-depth explanations of difficult concepts such as rebirth and nibbāna.

While I was undertaking the writing of this translation, some of my students recommended that I write in simpler language in order that the book might have a more general appeal. However, it is not easy to express the deeper significance of the Buddha's teachings in everyday language; the precise sense and depth of meaning can only be preserved in traditional terms, including the use of Pāli expressions where appropriate. The content of the book, insofar as it deals with the central themes of Buddhism, bears rereading in any case. In so doing, the reader will gain a richer understanding of the sutta and Buddhism more generally.

The primary contribution of this book is the manner of presentation of the translation of the original sutta, being couched in easily understood language. Each paragraph explains its particular subject matter according to the traditional scriptures. However, the reader is to understand that the Noble Eightfold Path is not only to be understood intellectually, but is also to be comprehended by way of practice. There are many people who practice vipassanā meditation under the direction of different teachers with different techniques. The explanations given in this book are devoid of sectarian thought.

Acknowledgments

THERE ARE MANY PEOPLE who helped me in writing this book and to whom I would like to express my particular thanks. Foremost, Yann Lovelock and Dr. Mar Mar Lwin were most helpful and their support was greatly appreciated. Also, I very much appreciate and am grateful to Bodhidhamma Bhikkhu and Margery Lamont who read and edited the final draft. I would also like to express special thanks to the Venerable Sumedho Bhikkhu, who wrote the foreword and inspired me greatly. And last, but certainly not least, my thanks to Denys Richards without whose support and help it would have been impossible for me to finish this work.

Finally, I would like to extend my sincere thanks and gratitude to Wisdom Publications. By publishing this book, Wisdom Publications is enabling the book to reach a wide readership. I am also most appreciative of Dr. Mar Mar Lwin's further financial support in contributing to the printing costs of this publication.

May all beings be well and happy.

U Rewata Dhamma
Buddhist Vihara
Birmingham, England

Publisher's Acknowledgment

The publisher gratefully acknowledges the generous support of the Birmingham Buddhist Vihara in helping to sponsor the production of this book.

Introduction

THE REASON FOR THE POPULARITY of the *Dhammacakka Sutta*, or the *Wheel of Dhamma Discourse*, among Theravādins is that it was the first sermon the Buddha gave after his enlightenment and is recognized as the foundation of all the Buddha's teachings. This book is essentially a commentary on that sutta. In order to help the reader, the presentation of the contents of the book mirrors the outline of the contents of the sutta. Chapter One begins with a review of the Buddha's life, telling how he was born as a royal prince and lived in luxury until his renunciation at the age of twenty-nine. The Buddha then practiced austerities for six years under the guidance of prominent teachers in India. This chapter explains very briefly how the Buddha practiced these austerities with the aim of attaining *nibbāna* (enlightenment). After a six-year struggle, the Buddha realized that the practice of self-mortification is too extreme (one of two extremes, actually), and he decided to undertake instead a more moderate path, the Middle Way. Soon after this he became enlightened.

At the time of the Buddha in India, there were six main principal philosophers and religious leaders—all of them wandering ascetics—who were presenting their respective teachings. The Buddha presented his teachings as a response to the prevalent religious and philosophical climate of his time. During his lifetime, he endeavored to abolish the caste system. He tirelessly campaigned against animal sacrifices, emphasizing in his teaching loving-kindness and compassion toward all beings.

The Buddha taught the doctrine of *kamma* (Skt. *karma*), which is the law of cause and effect. According to the Buddha, a person is the architect of his or her own destiny. It is unnecessary, therefore, to seek help from external agents, such as gods and goddesses. The Buddha advocated freedom of religion, freedom of thought, and, by today's measure, democratic principles for a harmonious society.

Chapter Two contains the translation of the *Dhammacakka Sutta*. The discourse describes the two extremes and the Middle Way, known as the Eightfold Path. By practicing the Eightfold Path, one realizes the Four Noble Truths. The Buddha proclaimed himself to be enlightened after he realized the Four Noble Truths.

The next five chapters comprise an exposition of this First Discourse.

Chapter Three tells of the Buddha's meeting with the five ascetics in Deer Park. He preached to them of the two extremes—indulgence in sensual pleasures and self-mortification—and of the Middle Path between these two. Chapter Four contains a detailed explanation of the Noble Eightfold Path. The definition of each aspect of the Path is offered from the traditional scriptures, as well as an explanation as to how the Noble Eightfold Path can be understood in relation to one's own meditation practice. Chapter Five deals with the Four Noble Truths: suffering, the origin of suffering, the cessation of suffering, and the path leading to the cessation of suffering. The Buddha identified the universal experiences of birth, decay, and death as suffering. One who attains the highest state of insight and has eradicated all traces of defilements becomes an *arahant.* Chapter Six sets out the seven stages of purification by means of which meditators strive to attain insight. In an effort to help the reader in understanding his or her own meditation experiences, an explanation of the three kinds of profound knowledge is included here, as well as further commentary on the threefold path in relation to vipassanā practice. The seventh chapter explains the twelve aspects of wisdom. Each of the Four Noble Truths has three types of knowledge or truth: the knowledge of the truth, the knowledge of the function of the truth, and the knowledge of the function of the truth that has been performed.

I close the last chapter by relating the acclamation of the discourse by the deities and by explaining the way of attainment of insight by the five ascetics who listened to the Buddha's first sermon, the *Wheel of Dhamma Discourse,* in Deer Park. At the end of the discourse, they applauded the Buddha's teachings and their wisdom eyes opened. They asked the Buddha to accept them into the order of monks so that they might live the holy life. The Buddha accepted their request and said, "Come and practice the holy life for the sake of the complete ending of suffering."

I have also included a glossary to assist the reader who may be unfamiliar with the Pāli terms.

1

Background

A unique being, an extraordinary man arises in this world for the benefit of the many, for the happiness of the many, out of compassion for the world, for the good, benefit, and happiness of devas and human beings. Who is this unique being? It is the Tathāgata, the exalted, fully enlightened one.

Anguttara Nikāya, 1.22

Well expounded is the Dhamma by the exalted one, to be self-realized, with immediate fruit, inviting investigation, leading on to Nibbāna, to be comprehended by the wise, each for himself.

Majjhima Nikāya, 1.37

The Life of the Buddha

In the year 623 B.C.E., on the full-moon day of May, the *bodhisatta* (future Buddha) was born in the kingdom of Kapilavatthu on the border of present-day India and Nepal. Born into the royal Sakya clan, he was given the name of Siddhattha, meaning "one whose purpose has been achieved." He received the conventional prince's education, which included training in the use of arms, extempore composition, and knowledge of polite deportment rules (which he subsequently incorporated into the conduct rules for monks and nuns in his order). He lived a life of luxury.

> I was delicate, excessively delicate. In my father's dwelling three lotus-ponds were made purposely for me. Blue lotuses bloomed in one, red in another, and white in another. I used no sandalwood that was not of Kāsī. My turban, tunic, dress and cloak, were all from Kāsi...
>
> Night and day a white parasol was held over me so that I might not be touched by heat or cold, dust, leaves or dew.
>
> There were three palaces for me: one for the cold season, one for the hot season, and one for the rainy season. During the four rainy months, I lived in the palace for the rainy season without ever coming down from it, entertained the while by female musicians.[1]

Although it is nowhere mentioned in the scriptures, it has been conjectured that the royal court supported the Sāṃkhya teachings, a non-Vedic philosophy connected with the early schools of Yoga and described later by Patañjali in his treatise, the *Yoga Sūtra.* There can be no doubt that Siddhattha practiced some form of contemplation while he was still young and at the age of twenty-nine, he became convinced of the unsatisfactoriness of his life. The future Buddha reflected thus:

> Youth, the prime of life, ends in old age and man's senses fail him when they are most needed. The hale and hearty lose their vigor and health when disease suddenly creeps in. Finally death comes, sudden perhaps and unexpected, and puts an end to this brief span of life. Surely there must be an escape from this unsatisfactoriness, from aging and death.[2]

So came about the event that came to be known as the great renunciation. The palace was no longer a congenial place for Siddhattha. Neither his beautiful wife nor newborn son could hold him back. He was destined for an infinitely more important and beneficial role than that of a dutiful husband or even a king of kings. He left secretly at midnight assuming the garb of a religious wanderer in search of the highest truth.

Meeting with the Great Teachers

Eventually the bodhisatta came to hear of the great teacher Āḷāra the Kālāma, who lived with three hundred pupils in Vesālī (or Vaisālī, now in the state of Bihar). He described their encounter as follows:

> Having gone forth and become a recluse in pursuit of what is holy and good, seeking the supreme, incomparable peace of nibbāna, I drew near to where Āḷāra the Kālāma was and addressed him thus: "Friend Kālāma, I desire to lead the holy life under your doctrine and discipline." Then Kālāma replied, "Friend Gotama Siddhattha is welcome to remain in this teaching. Of such a nature is this Dhamma that in a short time an intelligent man can realize for himself and abide in possession of what his teacher has realized as his own."[3]

What impressed the bodhisatta was Āḷāra's avoidance of quotation from scripture or from other teachers and his insistence that a doctrine is trustworthy and convincing only if it can be realized by oneself and in this lifetime. He thought to himself that it was not by mere faith that Āḷāra announced that he had learned the Dhamma. He felt that Āḷāra had surely realized the Dhamma for himself, that he knew and understood it.

What Āḷāra the Kālāma was teaching was a form of contemplative yoga. Instructed by him, the bodhisatta practiced diligently and quickly realized the "realm of nothingness," an advanced stage of concentration. His generous teacher was delighted to hear of his success and treated him as an equal, but the bodhisatta himself was not satisfied with this attainment. It did not lead to detachment, cessation of suffering, tranquillity, intuition, enlightenment, and nibbāna. Nor was he anxious to lead a religious school. He therefore went on to practice under Udaka Rāmaputta, another teacher of yoga contemplation, and achieved similar but not better results.

The bodhisatta reported to Udaka his attainment of the final stage or realm in the practice of *jhāna*, or meditative absorption, the realm of "neither perception nor nonperception." The sage Udaka told him that he was delighted and that the bodhisatta could proceed no further in the path. Like his former teacher Āḷāra, Udaka honored the bodhisatta by inviting him to take full charge of all the disciples as their teacher.

> Happy friend, we are extremely happy, in that we see such a venerable fellow-ascetic as you! The doctrine which ascetic Rāma knew, you know; the doctrine which you know, ascetic Rāma knew. As was Rāma so you are; as you are, so was Rāma. Come friend, henceforth you shall lead this company of ascetics.[4]

At the time of meeting with the bodhisatta, Udaka himself had not attained the realm of neither perception nor nonperception. He told the bodhisatta that only the ascetic Rāma had achieved it. So, when the bodhisatta proved himself to be the equal of his master, he offered the bodhisatta the leadership, and practicing under the bodhisatta's guidance, he himself attained the highest jhānic state of neither perception nor nonperception.

The Practice of Austerity

The bodhisatta remained leader of the community for a short while. Soon it occurred to him that this highest state of absorption was not what he yearned for. It did not lead to detachment, cessation of suffering, tranquillity, intuition, enlightenment, and nibbāna. He realized that the highest truth is to be found within oneself, and he ceased seeking external assistance. It was then that the bodhisatta decided that his quest must be an individual one. He settled in the Uruvela forest, near the market town of Senāni in the country of Magadha. Although he was to practice austerities, the spot itself was attractive, with the flowing Nerañjarā River, a pleasant sandy ford, a charming forest grove, and a village nearby that would serve as a place to beg alms. Then he thought thus:

> Lovely indeed is this spot of ground, charming is the forest grove, pleasant is the flowing river with sandy fords, and nearby is the village where I could obtain food. Suitable indeed is this place for spiritual exertion for those noble sons who desire to strive.[5]

Having heard about the bodhisatta's renunciation, a brāhmaṇa named Kondañña, who had prophesied Siddhattha's future buddhahood at his birth, came to the forest along with four friends—Bhaddiya, Vappa, Mahānāma, and Assaji—to practice austerities in the company of Siddhattha. These five young seekers would eventually become the Buddha's first disciples and would listen as the Buddha taught the *Dhammacakka Sutta* in Deer Park at Isipatana (present-day Sarnath) near Varanasi.

The Buddha mentions only two austerities that he practiced during that period. One was a form of breath retention which has extremely painful physiological results. The other was abstinence from food so extreme that he was reduced to almost a skeleton. The Buddha describes this practice to the wanderer, Aggivessana.

> I, Aggivessana, with my teeth clenched, with my tongue pressed against the palate, my mind should subdue, dominate, and restrain my mind. While I was subduing, restraining, and dominating my mind, with teeth clenched, the tongue pressed against the palate, sweat poured from my armpit. It is as if, Aggivessana, a strong man, having taken hold of a weaker man by his head or shoulders, would subdue, restrain, and dominate him. Nevertheless, Aggivessana, unsluggish energy came to be stirred up in me, unmuddled mindfulness set up, yet my body was turbulent, not calmed, because I was harassed by striving against that very pain. But, yet, Aggivessana, that painful feeling arising in me persisted without impinging on my mind.
>
> It occurred to me, Aggivessana: Suppose now that I should meditate

the non-breathing meditation? So I, Aggivessana, stopped breathing in and out through the mouth and through the nose. When I, Aggivessana, had stopped breathing, there came to be an exceedingly loud noise of wind escaping by the auditory passages, as there comes to be an exceedingly loud noise from the roaring of a smith's bellows. Nevertheless my energy was strenuous. Such painful sensations did not affect my mind. It occurred to me again that I should still meditate the non-breathing meditation. So I, Aggivessana, stopped breathing in and out through the mouth and through the nose and through the ears. And then exceedingly loud winds rent my head. As a strong man might cleave one's head with a sharp-edged sword. Nevertheless my energy was strenuous. Such painful sensations did not affect my mind. It occurred to me again that I should still meditate the non-breathing meditation. So I, Aggivessana, stopped breathing as before, I came to have very bad headaches, as a strong man might clamp a turban on one's head with a tight leather strap. Nevertheless my energy was strenuous. Such painful sensations did not affect my mind.

It occurred to me again that I should still meditate the non-breathing meditation. So I, Aggivessana, stopped breathing as before, then very strong winds cut through my stomach, as a skilled cattle butcher or his apprentice might cut through the stomach with a sharp butcher's knife. Nevertheless my energy was strenuous. Such painful sensations did not affect my mind. It occurred to me again that I should still meditate the non-breathing meditation. So I, Aggivessana, stopped breathing as before. Then there came to be a fierce heat in my body, as two strong men, having taken hold of a weaker man by his limbs, might set fire to him, might make him sizzle up over a charcoal pit. Nevertheless my energy was strenuous and indomitable. My mindfulness was established and unperturbed. Yet my body was fatigued and was not calmed as a result of that painful endeavor being overpowered by exertion, even though such painful sensations did not at all affect my mind.[6]

Abstinence from Food

Then, Aggivessana, the following thought occurred to me: I should take food little by little, a small quantity of the juice of green gram, or vetch, or lentils, or peas! As I took such a small quantity of solid and liquid food, my body became extremely emaciated. Just as are the joints of knot-grasses or bulrushes, even so were the major and minor parts of my body owing to lack of food. Just as is the camel's hoof, even so were my hips for want of food. Just as is a string of beads, even so did my backbone stand out and bend in for lack of food. Just as the rafters of a dilapidated hall fall this way and that, even so appeared my ribs through lack of sustenance. Just as in a deep well may be seen stars sunk deep in the water, even so did my eyeballs appear deep sunk in their sockets being devoid of food. Just as a bitter pumpkin, when cut while raw, will by wind and sun get shriveled and withered, even so did the skin of my head get shriveled and withered, due to lack of sustenance.

And I, Aggivessana, intending to touch my belly's skin, would instead seize my backbone. When I intended to touch my backbone, I would seize my belly's skin. So was I that, owing to lack of sufficient food, my belly's skin clung to the backbone, and I, on going to pass excreta or urine, would in that very spot stumble and fall down, for want of food. And I stroked my limbs in order to revive my body. Lo, as I did so, the rotten roots of my body's hairs fell from my body owing to lack of sustenance. To such an extent was the pure color of my skin impaired owing to lack of food.

Then, Aggivessana, the following thought occurred to me: Whatsoever ascetics or brāhmaṇas of the past have experienced acute, painful, sharp, and piercing sensations, they must have experienced them to such a high degree as this and not beyond. Whatsoever ascetics and brāhmaṇas of the future will experience acute, painful, sharp, and piercing sensations they too will experience them to such a high degree and not beyond. Yet by all these bitter and difficult austerities I shall not attain to excellence, worthy of supreme knowledge and insight, transcending those of human states. Might there be another path for enlightenment![7]

The Middle Path

Having realized the limitations of practicing such austerities and recalling the peace of his earlier contemplative practice in Kapilavatthu, the bodhisatta resolved to find a more balanced approach. However, with a body so utterly weakened as his he knew he could not yet follow this path with any chance of success. He therefore began to take enough food to restore his health and strength. Seeing this, the five disciples who had been attending him left in disappointment, believing that he had given up the quest in order to return to a life of comfort.

The bodhisatta was resolved to make his final search in complete solitude. He sat cross-legged under the Bodhi tree on the bank of the river Nerañjarā and made the final effort with the inflexible resolution: "Though only my skin, sinews, and bones remain, and my blood and flesh dry up and wither away, yet will I never stir from this seat until I have attained full enlightenment."[8]

Soon after applying mindfulness on in- and out-breathing (*ānāpānasati*), the bodhisatta entered upon and achieved the first meditative absorption, or jhāna. As he continued his practice he gained the second, third, and fourth stages. By developing the jhānas he gained perfect one-pointedness of mind. Thus cleansing his mind of impurities, he directed it to the knowledge of recollecting past births (*pubbenivāsānussatiñāṇa*). This, indeed, was the first knowledge, which he realized in the first watch of the night (6:00 P.M. to 10:00 P.M.). Then the bodhisatta directed his mind to the knowledge of the disappearing and reappearing of beings of varied forms, in good states of existence and in states of woe, all faring according to their deeds (*cuti-upapattiñāṇa*). This was the second knowledge, which he realized in the second watch of the night (10:00 P.M. to 2:00 A.M.). He then directed his mind to the knowledge of the destruction of the taints (*āsavakkhayañāṇa*) and perceived:

> This is dukkha; this is the 'arising of dukkha' (*dukkhasamudaya*); this is the 'cessation of dukkha' (*dukkhanirodha*); this is the 'path leading to the cessation of dukkha' (*dukkhanirodhagāminī paṭipadā*). Likewise, he understood as it really is: These are taints (*āsava*), this is the 'arising of taints' (*āsavasamudaya*), this is the 'cessation of taints' (*āsavanirodha*), this is the 'path leading to the cessation of taints' (*āsavanirodhagāminī paṭipadā*).[9]

Knowing thus, seeing thus, his mind was liberated from the taints of sense pleasures (*kāmāsava*), from the taints of becoming (*bhavāsava*), and from the taints of ignorance (*avijjāsava*). His mind was liberated; he realized, "Rebirth is ended. Fulfilled is the holy life. Done what was to be done. There is no more of this state again."[10]

This was the third knowledge attained by him in the last watch of the night (2:00 A.M. to 6:00 A.M.). Thus did Siddhattha Gotama, the bodhisatta, on the full-moon day of May, at the age of thirty-five, attain supreme enlightenment, by comprehending the Four Noble Truths in their fullness. Therein did he become a Buddha, a fully enlightened or awakened one.[11]

The Buddha then spoke these words of victory:

> Being subject to birth, aging, disease, death, sorrow, and defilement; seeing danger in what is subject to these things; seeking the unborn, unaging, diseaseless, deathless, sorrowless, undefiled, supreme security from bondage—nibbāna, I attained it. Knowledge and vision arose in me; unshakable is my deliverance of mind. This is the last birth, now there is no more becoming, no more rebirth.[12]

After attaining enlightenment, the Buddha sat for a week in the same posture at the foot of the Bodhi tree experiencing the bliss of deliverance. He contemplated dependent arising, or causal genesis (*paṭiccasamuppāda*). The Buddha then spent six more weeks in solitary retreat at six different places in the vicinity of the Bodhi tree.[13]

At the end of the seven weeks, he made up his mind to teach his first sermon to someone who would quickly grasp it. He considered Āḷāra the Kālāma who was learned, clever, wise, and had for long been with little dust in his eyes. However, through his supernormal vision it became clear to the Buddha that Āḷāra the Kālāma had passed away just seven days before. Then he thought of the hermit Udaka, son of the great sage Rāma. But through his supernormal vision he realized that the hermit Udaka had died only the evening before.

Finally, he thought of the five energetic ascetics who had attended him during his struggle for enlightenment. With his supernormal vision he perceived that they were residing in Deer Park at Isipatana, the resort of seers, near Varanasi. He then left the *bodhimaṇḍala* (vicinity of the Bodhi tree) for Isipatana, in the vicinity of Varanasi, to teach his first sermon, the *Wheel of Dhamma Discourse.*

Meeting with Upaka

On the road to Varanasi, near the city of Gayā, the Buddha met a wandering ascetic named Upaka. Upaka addressed the Buddha thus: "Oh friend, your senses are extremely clear, and your complexion is pure and clean. Friend, on account of whom has your renunciation been made? Who is your teacher?" The Buddha replied:

> All have I overcome, all do I know,
> From all am I detached, all have I renounced.
> Wholly absorbed am I in the destruction of craving.
> Having comprehended all by myself, whom shall I call my teacher?

No teacher have I. An equal to me there is not.
In the world including gods there is no rival to me.
Indeed an arahant am I in this world. An unsurpassed teacher am I;
Alone am I, the all-enlightened. Cool and appeased am I.
To establish the wheel of Dhamma to the city of Kāsi go I.
In this blind world I shall beat the drum of deathlessness.[14]

SOCIAL AND PHILOSOPHICAL CONTEXT OF THE BUDDHA'S LIFETIME

The Buddha taught in northeast India, along the valley of the river Ganges, where Brahmanism (the early form of today's Hinduism) was the dominant religion. Brahmanism taught that escape from transmigration, or the salvation of the soul (*ātman*), could only be attained by the due performance of Vedic sacrifices, observances of religious rites, ceremonies, and the offering of gifts to brāhmaṇas (or priests). Society was divided into four castes: brāhmaṇas, kṣatriyas (warriors), vaiśyas (cultivators), and śudras (servants). Caste membership was determined by birth, and occupation and social standing were fixed very strictly throughout life according to one's caste. Brahmanism taught the doctrine of kamma in a limited sense, such that the conditions of one's rebirth depended on sacrificial deeds performed during one's life.

The primary scriptures of Brahmanism, called the *Vedas*, are collections of invocations to deities in the form of hymns and prayers. They were recited at Vedic sacrificial rituals, which brāhmaṇas performed with the aim of increasing wealth and progeny, defeating enemies, and so on. The philosophical stance of the Vedas is not very clear, but it does seem to support the notion of a creator god, known as Prajāpati. It is characteristic of all later forms of Brahmanism and Hinduism that the Vedas are held as sacred and eternal. Over time, the followers of the Vedas composed new treatises, known as the *brāhmaṇas*. Together, the Vedas and the Brāhmaṇas comprised the corpus known as *Śruti*.

At this time in India there were many forest dwellers and sages who were seeking for spiritual understanding; the conversations that took place between such sages and their pupils are recorded in the *Upaniṣads*. The main teachings of these texts were that the absolute reality, or Brahman, is identical to the individual soul, or ātman. The ātman does not realize that it is Brahman because it is entangled in illusion (*māyā*). When the ātman realizes its true identity through meditation, it becomes free from the beginningless cycle of transmigrations and attains salvation.

Kapila the Rationalist

Contemporary to the teachers of the *Upaniṣads* was the unique philosopher Kapila. His system, known as the Sāṃkhya system, was of a startling nature. According to him, truth must be supported by proof in the form of either perception or inference. There is no truth without proof. Kapila denied the theory of the creation of the universe by a being or god. He said that the empirical universe consists of manifest things (*vyakta*) and unmanifest things (*avyakta*). Both the manifest and the unmanifest have a cause, but that cause itself is independent and uncaused. Kapila taught the two fundamentals of self (*puruṣa*) and nature (*prakṛti*), or subject and object. All experience is based on the duality of the subject and object. Kapila also speaks of three constituents (*guṇas*): lightness (*sattva*), motion (*rajas*), and heaviness (*tamas*). These three are like the constituents of a lamp—the flame, oil, and wick. When the three guṇas are in perfect balance, none overpowering the others, the universe appears to be static (*acetana*) and ceases to become manifest. When they are not in balance, one overpowers the others, and the universe becomes dynamic (*sacetana*) and becomes manifest. Kapila maintained that the cause of imbalance was suffering, or dukkha.

Non-Brāhmaṇic Teachers

The sixth century B.C.E. in India was a time remarkable for its spiritual unrest, intellectual foment, and changing social conditions. There were wandering sages (*samaṇas*) who rejected the traditional Vedic concepts of sacrificial rituals practiced by brāhmaṇas. There were also naked ascetics (*ājīvakas*) who likewise condemned traditional Brahmanism. Sixty-two schools of philosophy are reputed to have opposed traditional Brahmanism.

In the Buddhist scriptures, frequent reference is made to six contemporaries of the Buddha, each of whom was a founder of a religious school with a large following. Their names and the particular doctrines they held are briefly stated in the Buddhist texts. Most of the essential doctrines of these six schools were rejected by the Buddha. A brief elaboration of these six philosophical schools is therefore illuminating for an understanding of the Buddha's own teachings.

1. The doctrine of non-action (*akiriyavāda*), taught by Purāṇa Kassapa, maintained that the soul was not affected in any way by kamma. Neither unwholesome nor wholesome actions have any effect (*kiriya*) on the soul. When a person dies, all the elements of which the person is made return to their original state. Nothing survives after death, neither body nor soul.

2. The doctrine of fate or destiny (*niyativāda*), propounded by Makkhali Ghosāla, was a kind of fatalism or philosophical determinism. He argued that no one can do anything or undo anything. Things happen by themselves; no one can make them happen. No one can remove unhappiness, nor increase nor diminish it. One must undergo one's share of experiences of the world. Makkhali Ghosāla belonged to a sect of naked ascetics (*acelaka*). He taught that liberation is attained only by passing through all kinds of existences. He did not believe that there was any special cause either for the misery of human beings nor for their deliverance and he held that all beings were helpless against destiny. According to him, all beings, whether wise or foolish, were destined to pass through the cycle of rebirth (*saṁsāra*), and their misery would end at the completion of the cycle. No human effort could reduce or lengthen this period. Saṁsāra had a fixed term through which every being must pass.

3. The doctrine of nihilism (*ucchedavāda*), expounded by Ajita Kesakambala, taught that sacrifice and offerings had no effect whatsoever. There was no such thing as the result or effect of deeds to be enjoyed or suffered by the soul. There is neither heaven nor hell. Man was made of certain elements, into which the body dissolved after death. Ajita Kesakambala also held that it was useless to talk about the next world; both the wise and the ignorant die and have no future life after death.

4. The doctrine of "one or the other" (*aññoñavāda*), preached by Pakudha Kaccāyana, was also a kind of doctrine of non-action (*akiriyavāda*). According to this doctrine, there are seven elements that make up a being, namely: earth, water, fire, air, happiness, unhappiness, and soul. Each element is independent of the others and they do not affect one another. They exist independently and they are eternal. Nothing can destroy them. If a man chops off the head of another man he does not kill him. The weapon has simply entered the seven elements. According to Pakudha Kaccāyana, the seven elements are immutable and do not in any way contribute to pleasure or pain. The body is ultimately dissolved into these eternal elements.

5. The doctrine of skepticism (*vikkhepavāda*) was a subtle philosophy taught by Sañjaya Belaputta. Sañjaya Belaputta argued, "Were someone to ask me if there is a heaven, if I felt there was I would say 'yes.' But if I felt there was no heaven, then I would say 'no.' If I am asked whether human beings are created, whether man has to suffer the result of his actions, good or bad, and whether the soul lives on after death, I say nay to all because I

do not think they exist." Sañjaya Belaputta always declined to give categorical answers to problems facing the human mind.

6. The doctrine of restraint of four precepts (*catuyāmasaṃvaravāda*) was preached by Nigaṇṭhanāthaputta, who was also known as Mahāvira. This is the only one of the six schools which still survives today. In India and elsewhere it is the religious tradition known as Jainism. Mahāvira, the founder, or according to Jain tradition, the last prophet of the present world cycle, seems to have been slightly older than the Buddha. He taught ethical doctrines similar to those of the ascetic Pārasvanāth, his predecessor by about 250 years. Jains believe that the soul has to undergo rebirth because of the bad kamma incurred in the past life and the present life. Mahāvira prescribed five moral precepts in terms of four restraints (*catuyāmasaṁvara*): (1) not to kill; (2) not to steal; (3) not to tell lies; and (4) not to own property and to observe celibacy. He said that by observing the precepts one prevents bad kamma. According to Jains, however, Jainism is not only an ethical system, but also a philosophy based on the doctrine of many possibilities (*anekāntavāda*).

THE BUDDHA'S DHAMMA

> Therein, bhikkhu, when those recluses and brahmins who are eternalists proclaim on four grounds the self and the world to be eternal—that is only the feeling of those who do not know and do not see; that is only the agitation and vacillation of those who are immersed in craving.
>
> *Brahmajāla Sutta, Dīgha Nikāya, 1.13*

The teachings of the Buddha were frequently said to be against the grain (*patisotagāmi*) of the practices and beliefs current in his time. The truth that the Buddha realized when he attained enlightenment under the Bodhi tree did not correspond to the tenets of Brahmanism. In fact, the Buddha waged an energetic campaign against the Vedic practice of animal sacrifice, teaching instead the value of life and the benefit of cultivating loving-kindness and compassion toward all living beings. At the same time, the Buddha did not discover the truth through the teachings of any of his contemporaries who rejected Brahmanism, including the six most prominent of these who are described above. Rather, the Buddha looked directly into the nature of reality and discovered the reality of dependent origination (*paṭiccasamuppāda*).

In the words of the Venerable Assaji, spoken to Upatissa:

> Whatever from a cause proceeds, thereof
> The Tathāgata has explained the cause,
> Its cessation too he has explained.
> This is the teaching of the supreme sage.[15]

The Law of Kamma

The Buddha taught that there is an order to the physical world, that there is an order to the movements and actions of the starry bodies, an order by which seasons come and go in regular sequence, an order by which seeds grow into trees and trees yield fruits and fruits give seed. These are *niyāmas*, or universal laws, which produce an orderly sequence in nature. Similarly, there is a moral order in human society. According to the Buddha, this moral order is not maintained by a creator God, but is rather maintained by the *kammaniyāma*, or the law of action. If wholesome actions (*kusalakamma*) are performed, the moral order is good. If the moral order is bad it is because unwholesome actions (*akusalakamma*) have been undertaken. This is the universal law of kamma and *vipāka*; kamma refers to an individual's actions and vipāka refers to their result. According to this law, the effect of the deed is bound to follow the deed, as surely as night follows day.

The Buddha's doctrine of causal relations does not postulate merely a single cause for any given event. Rather, phenomena or events are the product of a multiplicity of causes or conditions. There is no single cause nor any first cause which conditions a particular effect. The question of the cause of a first event does not arise because a first event can never be discovered.

In Buddhism, proving the primary origin of things is not emphasized. The Buddha discouraged philosophical speculations, such as those that concern the origin of the world, the existence of a creator God, life after death, and so on, since they have nothing to do with overcoming human suffering. He gave the analogy of being wounded by an arrow. The first thing one must do is to remove the arrow. If instead one insists upon investigating who shot the arrow, from whence it came, what kind of arrow it was, and so on, one might die before ever finding the answers to such questions. Therefore, the Buddha emphasized that rather than engaging in useless speculations, one must understand the truth of suffering (*dukkha*) and the path for overcoming suffering.

Although the Buddha accepted that there is a moral order to the universe and that this order is based upon the universal law of action, he did not accept that this moral order in any way entailed the caste system of

Brāhmaṇic Hinduism. Rather, the Buddha denounced all claims to superiority on the grounds of birth and all social distinctions among humans. He declared that kamma, the actions of the individual, determines one's superiority or inferiority. Hence, the Buddha did not bar women or persons born into the lower castes from entry into the *sangha.*

The Buddha also rejected the notion, central to the Brāhmaṇic tradition, that there existed an everlasting self, soul, or ātman. He asked his disciples to investigate the substantiality of the self through vipassanā meditation. Under the scrutiny of the observational powers of vipassanā, one can discover for oneself that the self which one thinks is permanent is, in reality, made up of five physical and mental aggregates, and that all these aggregates are continuously changing. Nothing remains the same for even two consecutive moments. Everything is impermanent. The Buddha said that whatever is impermanent (*anicca*) is suffering (*dukkha*); and he said that whatever is impermanent is also devoid of self or essence (*anatta*). To teach this profound realization he said:

> All compounded things (*dhammas*) are impermanent and suffering.
> All things, whether compounded or uncompounded,
> Are free from self or essence; when one sees this with wisdom,
> One becomes dispassionate toward dukkha.
> This is the path of purification.[16]

Like Kapila, the Buddha also stressed that reality must rest on proof, that thinking must be based on rationalism, and that there is suffering in the world. He rejected the notion of a God and a God-created universe as having no logical or factual basis. He rejected the extremes of indulgence in sense objects and self-mortification, saying that these lead to materialistic views of eternalism, on the one hand, and nihilism on the other. The Buddha advocated following the Middle Path free from these extremes.

The teaching of the Buddha can be summed up in the word "Dhamma." This word means "truth," or "that which really is." Dhamma also means law, the law that exists in a human being's heart and mind; it is the principle of righteousness existing not only in human beings but in the universe as well. All the universe is a revelation of Dhamma. The Buddha appealed to human beings to be noble, pure, and charitable, not in order to please any supreme deity but to be true to the highest truth within themselves. If one lives in accordance with Dhamma one may well escape suffering and realize nibbāna. However, until one is able to still the storm in one's heart and extend compassion to all beings, one will not be able to take even the first step toward this end.

The Buddha taught that all human beings have the potential to become a buddha if they so aspire. Buddhas arise as a result of their own efforts and practice over many lifetimes, and not on account of some external power. A buddha is a man par excellence (*purisuttama*), living the life of a human being outwardly, but inwardly he is transcendent.

> Even as, monks, a lotus born and grown in muddy water stands above, unsmeared by the muddy water, so is the Tathāgata, monks, born and grown up in the world, yet lives lord over the world without coming together with the world.[17]

According to the Buddha, human beings are masters of their own destiny. He encouraged his disciples to seek refuge within themselves, to find the way to free themselves from bondage to suffering through effort and intelligence. He showed the way to liberation, nibbāna.

> Oneself is one's own refuge; what other refuge can there be?
> Purity and impurity depend on oneself. No one can purify another.[18]

The Position of Humans

In his first sermon, the Buddha taught the Middle Path, the path free from the two extremes of sensual indulgence and self-mortification, or excessive ascetic practices (which he himself had followed before discovering the Middle Path). The Middle Path is a practical approach to freeing oneself from suffering and attaining enlightenment. The Buddha attributed all his realizations, attainments, and achievements to human endeavor and practice. The Buddhadhamma is applicable to all classes of men and women: kings and peasants, high castes and low castes, bankers and beggars, holy men and robbers, with no distinction between them. The path is open to all those who are ready to understand and follow the Dhamma. The Buddha emphasized that he was only a guide to show people the path (*maggadātā*) and not one who could give salvation (*mokkhadātā*). He spoke of individual responsibility. He encouraged and stimulated each person to develop himself or herself to work out their own emancipation, to liberate themselves from bonds through their own personal effort and intelligence.

> You should work for your own liberation,
> for the Tathāgatas only show the way.[19]

Freedom of Religion

The Buddha advised his followers to respect all other religious orders. Upāli, for instance, a prominent, wealthy householder and well-known lay disciple of Nigaṇṭha Nāthaputta, became convinced that the teachings of the Buddha were right and those of his teacher wrong. He begged the Buddha to accept him as one of his lay disciples (*upāsaka*). However, the Buddha asked him to reconsider and not to be rash, for, "considering carefully is good for well-known men like you." When Upāli reiterated his desire, the Buddha accepted him but requested that he continue to respect and support his old religious teachers as he was accustomed to doing.[20]

General Sīha of Vesālī was also a disciple of Nigaṇṭha Nāthaputta, who, after conversing with the Buddha, declared himself his follower. But the Buddha accepted him only on the understanding that Sīha would continue to support his former teacher. This attitude of the Buddha made Sīha respect the Buddha even more.[21] The Buddha stressed tolerance. His teachings were intended to be a unifying, not divisive, force in society.

The Path of Purification

Strictly speaking, Buddhism is not a religion in the sense commonly understood. It is a path of purification open to all without discrimination. The Buddha is neither savior, prophet, nor god. One need not accept the Buddha personally to attain salvation. The Buddha taught out of compassion toward all living beings. He taught that greed, anger, and delusion are latent mental dispositions in the human mind. Because of greed, anger, and delusion, one cannot discriminate right from wrong and consequently one undertakes unwholesome actions. If the mind is pure, influenced by loving-kindness (*mettā*), compassion (*karunā*), and wisdom (*paññā*), one's actions also become pure and wholesome.

> Not to do any evil, to cultivate good,
> to purify one's mind. This is the teaching of the buddhas.[22]

The Buddha stressed that the first thing we must do is seek light to dispel the darkness of ignorance, which fuels the fire of greed and hatred.

> What is laughter, what is joy, when the world is ever burning?
> Shrouded by darkness would you not seek the light?[23]

2

The First Discourse of the Buddha: Turning the Wheel of Dhamma

Declared is the straight path, walk along, falter not;
Let each admonish himself, and by stages reach nibbāna.

Theragāthā, v. 637

I. THUS HAVE I HEARD: At one time the Blessed One was staying at Deer Park, in Isipatana (the Sage's Resort) near Varanasi.

The Two Extremes

II. Then the Buddha addressed the five ascetics: "O bhikkhus, one who has gone forth from worldly life should not indulge in these two extremes. What are the two? There is indulgence in desirable sense objects, which is low, vulgar, worldly, ignoble, unworthy, and unprofitable and there is devotion to self-mortification, which is painful, unworthy, and unprofitable.

The Middle Path

III. "O bhikkhus, avoiding both these extremes, the Tathāgata has realized the Middle Path. It produces vision, it produces knowledge, it leads to calm, to higher knowledge, to enlightenment, to nibbāna.

IV. "And what is that Middle Path, O bhikkhus, that the Tathāgata has realized? It is simply the Noble Eightfold Path, namely: Right understanding, right thought, right speech, right action, right livelihood, right effort, right awareness, and right concentration. This is the Noble Eightfold Path realized by the Tathāgata. It produces vision, it produces knowledge, it leads to calm, to higher knowledge, to enlightenment, to nibbāna.

The Four Noble Truths

V. "This, O bhikkhus, is the Noble Truth of suffering (*dukkha*): Birth is suffering, aging is suffering, sickness is suffering, death is suffering, sorrow, and lamentation, pain, grief, and despair are suffering,[24] association with the unloved or unpleasant condition is suffering, separation from the beloved or pleasant condition is suffering, not to get what one wants is suffering. In brief, the five aggregates of attachment are suffering.

VI. "This, O bhikkhus, is the Noble Truth of the origin of suffering: It is craving which produces rebirth, bound up with pleasure and greed. It finds delight in this and that, in other words, craving for sense pleasures, craving for existence or becoming and craving for nonexistence or self-annihilation.

VII. "This, O bhikkhus, is the Noble Truth of the cessation of suffering: It is the complete cessation of suffering; giving up, renouncing, relinquishing, detaching from craving.

VIII. "This, O bhikkhus, is the Noble Truth of the path leading to the cessation of suffering. It is simply the Noble Eightfold Path, namely: Right understanding, right thought, right speech, right action, right livelihood, right effort, right awareness, and right concentration.

Twelve Aspects of Wisdom

IX. "This is the Noble Truth of suffering. Thus, O bhikkhus, concerning things not heard before, there arose in me the vision, the knowledge, the wisdom, the insight, and the light.

X. "This is the Noble Truth of suffering, which should be fully understood. Thus, O bhikkhus, concerning things not heard before, there arose in me the vision, the knowledge, the wisdom, the insight, and the light.

XI. "This is the Noble Truth of suffering, which has been understood. Thus, O bhikkhus, concerning things not heard before, there arose in me the vision, the knowledge, the wisdom, the insight, and the light.

XII. "This is the Noble Truth of the Origin of Suffering. Thus, O bhikkhus, concerning things not heard before, there arose in me the vision, the knowledge, the wisdom, the insight, and the light.

XIII. "This is the Noble Truth of the origin of suffering, which should be abandoned. Thus, O bhikkhus, concerning things not heard by me before, there arose in me the vision, the knowledge, the wisdom, the insight, and the light.

XIV. "This is the Noble Truth of the origin of suffering, which has been abandoned. Thus, O bhikkhus, concerning things not heard before, there arose in me the vision, the knowledge, the wisdom, the insight, and the light.

XV. "This is the Noble Truth of the cessation of suffering. Thus, O bhikkhus, concerning things not heard before, there arose in me the vision, the knowledge, the wisdom, the insight, and the light.

XVI. "This is the Noble Truth of the cessation of suffering, which should be realized. Thus, O bhikkhus, concerning things not heard before, there arose in me the vision, the knowledge, the wisdom, the insight, and the light.

XVII. "This is the Noble Truth of the cessation of suffering, which has been realized. Thus, O bhikkhus, concerning things not heard before, there arose in me the vision, the knowledge, the wisdom, the insight, and the light.

XVIII. "This is the Noble Truth of the path leading to the cessation of suffering. Thus, O bhikkhus, concerning things not heard before, there arose in me the vision, the knowledge, the wisdom, the insight, and the light.

XIX. "This is the Noble Truth of the path leading to the cessation of suffering, which should be developed. Thus, O bhikkhus, concerning things not heard before, there arose in me the vision, the knowledge, the wisdom, the insight, and the light.

XX. "This is the Noble Truth of the path leading to the cessation of suffering, which has been developed. Thus, O bhikkhus, concerning things not heard before, there arose in me the vision, the knowledge, the wisdom, the insight, and the light.

Enlightenment Not Yet Claimed

XXI. "As long, O bhikkhus, as my vision of true knowledge was not fully clear in these three aspects and in these twelve ways regarding the Four Noble Truths, I did not claim to have realized the perfect enlightenment that is supreme in the world with its devas, māras and brahmās, in this world with its recluses and brāhmaṇas, with its princes and men.

Enlightenment Claimed

XXII. "But when, O bhikkhus, my vision of true knowledge was fully clear in these three aspects and in these twelve ways regarding the Four Noble Truths, then I claimed to have realized the perfect enlightenment that is supreme in the world with its devas, māras and brahmās, in this world with its recluses and brāhmaṇas, with its princes and men.

XXIII. "Indeed, a vision of true knowledge arose in me thus: My mind's deliverance is unassailable. This is the last birth. Now there is no more becoming."

Reflections on the Sermon

XXIV. Thus the Buddha spoke. The group of five bhikkhus was glad and acclaimed his words. While this doctrine was being expounded, there arose in the Venerable Kondañña the pure, immaculate vision of the truth and he realized, "Whatsoever is subject to causation is also subject to cessation."

XXV. When the Buddha expounded the discourse, thus putting into motion the turning of the wheel of Dhamma, the devas of the earth exclaimed: "This excellent wheel of Dhamma, which could not be expounded by any ascetic, brāhmaṇa, deva, māra or brahmā in this world, has been put into motion by the Blessed One at Deer Park, in Isipatana, near Varanasi."

Hearing this, the devas Catumahārājika, Tavatiṃsā, Yāmā, Tussitā, Nimmānarati, Paranimmitavasavati, and the brahmās of Brahmāpārisajjā, Brahmāpurohitā, Mahābrahmā, Parittābhā, Appamāṇabhā, Ābhassarā, Parittasubhā, Appamāṇasubhā, Subhakiṇṇā, Vehapphalā, Avihā, Atappā, Sudassā, Sudassī, and Akaniṭṭhā also raised the same joyous cry.

Thus, at that very moment, at that very instant, this joyous cry extended as far as the brahmā realm. These ten thousand world systems quaked, tottered, and trembled violently. A radiant light, surpassing the radiance of the devas appeared in the world.

XXVI. Then the Buddha said, "Friends, Kondañña has indeed understood. Friends, Kondañña has indeed understood." Therefore, the Venerable Kondañña was named Aññāsi Kondañña—"Kondañña who understands."

3

The Middle Way

This is the only way,
There is none other for the purity of vision;
Do you follow this path?
This is the bewilderment of the evil one (Māra).

Dhammapada, v.274

Nibbāna is no lie (no state unreal)
For it is known as truth by the noble ones.
But since they realize that truth
Desireless they pass away.

Suttanipāta, v.143

I. *Thus have I heard: At one time the Blessed One was staying at Deer Park in Isipatana (the Sage's Resort) near Varanasi.*

Every discourse in the Sutta Piṭaka is introduced with the words "Thus have I heard." These were the introductory words that the Venerable Ānanda uttered when questioned by the Venerable Mahākassapa at the First Council, which convened three months after the Buddha passed away. It was at this meeting of the sangha that the Buddha's teachings were first compiled together to be recited and committed to memory. The Venerable Ānanda was the first cousin of the Buddha and his personal attendant for twenty-five years. For the first twenty years of his enlightenment, the Buddha had no permanent attendant. This raises the question of how Ānanda heard those discourses which the Buddha delivered over the course of the first twenty years of his teaching.

It is said that when the Buddha asked Ānanda to become his attendant, Ānanda replied that he would accept the position only if the Blessed One agreed to the following eight conditions:

1. The Buddha must not give him any robes for being his attendant.
2. He should not be given good food received by the Buddha.
3. He should not be asked to stay in the Buddha's fragrant chamber, but have a separate cell for himself.

4. He should not be included if anyone invited the Buddha to visit his house and partake of food.
5. He must have the right to accept any invitation for the Buddha and, once he had accepted the invitation, the Buddha must go to that invited place.
6. He should be permitted, at any time, to bring to the Buddha a devotee coming from a far-off place.
7. He should be permitted to place before the Buddha any problem as soon as it arose.
8. The Buddha should repeat to him any discourse delivered in his absence.

The Buddha accepted these conditions before Ānanda agreed to be his attendant. According to the first four conditions, Ānanda did not want any material benefit from his relationship to the Buddha. The last condition is very important with respect to the words, "Thus have I heard," because the Buddha always repeated to Ānanda any discourse delivered in his absence. Therefore, the Venerable Ānanda knew all the discourses and teachings delivered by the Buddha during his forty-five years of teaching. After the passing away of the Buddha, the chief disciple, Mahākassapa, decided to hold a council for the future safety and purity of the Buddha's teachings. He asked Ānanda: "Friend, Ānanda, when was the wheel of Dhamma delivered? By whom was it delivered and on whose account? And how was it delivered?" Then Ānanda answered, "Venerable Mahākassapa, thus have I heard: At one time the Blessed One was staying at Deer Park, in Isipatana (the Sage's Resort) near Varanasi. Then the Buddha addressed the five ascetics..."

As in other suttas, there is no definite date to this discourse. Precise chronological data as to the year and the month in which each sutta was delivered would have been very helpful. But chronological details would be an encumbrance to committing the suttas to memory and to their recitation. Nevertheless, it is generally believed that the Buddha taught this discourse on the full-moon day of July, two months after his enlightenment.

Meeting with the Five Ascetics

The five ascetics who had attended the bodhisatta while he undertook austerity practices—Kondañña, Bhaddiya, Vappa, Mahānāma, and Assaji—lived in Deer Park, in Isipatana (the Sage's Resort). When the bodhisatta changed his method of practice from austerities to the Middle Path, the five ascetics had abandoned him, believing he had given up the quest. When they subsequently saw the Buddha, they decided not to pay him due respect as they had misconstrued his discontinuance of rigid ascetic practices. They made an agreement saying, "Friends, the ascetic Gotama is coming. He is luxurious. He has given up striving and has turned to a life of abundance. He should not be greeted and waited upon. His bowl and robe should not be taken. Nevertheless, a seat should be prepared. If he wishes, let him sit down." However, as the Buddha continued to draw near, his august personality was such that they were compelled to receive him with due honor. One came forward and took his bowl and robe, another prepared a seat, and yet another brought water for his feet. Nevertheless, they still addressed him by name and called him friend (*āvuso*) Gotama, a form of address applied generally to juniors and equals.

Then the Buddha said to them:

> Do not, O bhikkhus, address the Tathāgata by name or by the title 'friend.' An exalted one, O bhikkhus, is the Tathāgata. A fully enlightened one is he. Give ear, O bhikkhus! Deathlessness (*amata*) has been attained. I shall instruct and teach the Dhamma. If you act according to my instructions, you will before long realize, attaining in this life itself, by your own intuitive wisdom, that supreme consummation of the holy life, for the sake of which sons of noble families rightly leave home for homelessness.[25]

The five ascetics replied:

> By that demeanor of yours, friend Gotama, by that discipline, by those painful austerities, you did not attain to any superhuman specific knowledge and insight worthy of a noble one. How will you, when you have become luxurious, have given up striving, and have turned to a life of abundance, gain any such superhuman knowledge and insight worthy of a noble one?

The Buddha explained to them:

> The Tathāgata, O bhikkhus, is not luxurious, has not given up striving and has not turned to a life of abundance. An exalted one is the Tathāgata. A fully enlightened one is he. Give ear, O bhikkhus! Deathlessness has been attained. I shall instruct and teach the Dhamma.[26]

A second time the prejudiced ascetics expressed their disappointment in the same manner. A second time the Buddha reassured them of his attainment of enlightenment. When the adamant ascetics refused to believe him and expressed their view for the third time, the Buddha questioned them thus, "Do you know, O bhikkhus, of an occasion when I ever spoke to you thus before?" "Nay, indeed, Lord!" they replied. The Buddha repeated for the third time that he had gained enlightenment and that they also could realize the Dhamma if they would act according to his instructions. At that point they were convinced and sat in silence to listen.

AVOIDING THE TWO EXTREMES

> II. *Then the Buddha addressed the five ascetics: "O bhikkhus, one who has gone forth from worldly life should not indulge in these two extremes. What are the two? There is indulgence in desirable sense objects, which is low, vulgar, worldly, ignoble, unworthy, and unprofitable and there is devotion to self-mortification, which is painful, unworthy, and unprofitable."*

Because it was commonly believed that happiness or ultimate truth could only be experienced through extreme asceticism and self-mortification, the bodhisatta had also practiced various forms of austerities for six years before realizing their futility. The five ascetics firmly believed that without strict asceticism liberation was not possible. So the Buddha elaborated for them the two extremes to be avoided.

The first extreme was the indulgence in desirable sense objects (sight, sound, smell, taste, and touch). Taking delight in such objects of pleasure and enjoying them physically and mentally inclines one to pursue these sensuous pleasures. The Buddha experienced this extreme as a prince before renouncing sensual pleasures. The other extreme, involving attempts to inflict torture on oneself, could result only in suffering. Rejecting food and clothing, which one is normally used to, is a form of self-torture and is unprofitable. The renunciation of the worldly life does not necessarily mean an outright denial of life's supports.

Delighting in sensuous pleasures and relishing them is to be regarded as a vulgar practice. Such enjoyments lead to the formation of base desires—which are clinging and lustful—and tend to develop conceit and avarice. One who enjoys sensuous objects believes that no one else is in a position to enjoy such pleasure and does not wish to share the good fortune with others, or else is overcome by thoughts of jealousy. Indulgence in sensual pleasures does not suit those who have gone forth from the worldly life. This kind of practice is the concern of so-called 'urban civilization,' which condones sensuous pleasures as the highest attributes of bliss; the greater the pleasures, the greater the happiness. Paradoxically, insecurity, ill will, violence, and war are the end results of such an attitude.

There were people who held the belief that supreme bliss could be attained here and now (*diṭṭhadhammanibbānavāda*). According to them, sensual pleasure was blissful and should be enjoyed in this very life; it would be foolish to let precious moments of enjoyment pass, waiting for bliss in a future life that does not exist.[27]

The Buddha taught that indulgence in sensuous pleasures is not the practice of enlightened, noble ones (*ariyas*). Noble ones who live the worldly life do not have attachment to sense objects. For example, in the first stage of an enlightened noble life, the sotāpanna, or stream winner, has not yet overcome lust and passions. Incipient perceptions of the agreeableness of carnal pleasures (*sukhasaññā*) still linger. Nevertheless, the stream-winner will not feel the need to indulge in worldly pleasures.

Indulgence in sensual pleasures does not lead to one's own welfare or well-being. In general, accumulating wealth, establishing a family life, striving for success and prosperity in this world seem to mean working for one's own welfare. But, in reality, attaining such worldly success and prosperity does not amount to one's ultimate well-being. Striving for one's own welfare may condition greater or lesser well-being in the cycle of rebirths in *saṁsāra.* But this is not the way to overcome old age, disease and death, nor to free oneself from all forms of suffering. In order to eradicate suffering, one must practice morality (*sīla*), concentration (*samādhi*), and wisdom (*paññā*) to which the pursuit of sensual pleasures proves a hindrance.

Worldlings and Sensual Pleasures

The sutta says that one who has gone forth from the worldly life should not indulge in sensuous pleasures. The question, therefore, arises whether ordinary worldlings may freely enjoy sensual pleasures. Since the gratification of sense desires is a human preoccupation, the Buddha emphasized the Middle Path. When one lives amidst worldly surroundings, one can enjoy sensual pleasures with wisdom; but one should avoid habits which lead to craving. The householder whose practice is serious should try to rein in and diminish his or her desires and observe the third moral precept to abstain from misuse of the senses (*kāmesumicchācāra*).

Self-Mortification

Devotion to self-mortification is the opposite of sensual indulgence. It is a form of self-torture practiced under the belief that luxurious living causes attachment to sensual pleasures and that only extreme austerity could lead to eternal peace. Some of the practices performed by extreme ascetics included denial of food and clothing; immersion in frigid water during cold weather; and in hot weather, exposure to the sun or standing near burning fires. They did not use beds but, instead, took rest naked on the ground. Some resorted to lying on prickly thorns covered only by a sheet. Others remained in a sitting posture for days, or kept to standing only, neither lying nor sitting down. Some completely cut off food and water. There were some who ate on alternate days only, while others ate once in two or three days. Some even abstained from food and water for fifteen days on end. Some reduced their meal to just one handful of food, while others lived on nothing but green vegetables and grass or even cow excrement. The Buddha also practiced in this way during his six-year struggle before discovering the Middle Path.

The practice of self-mortification was regarded by naked ascetics as being a holy pursuit. Some naked ascetics at the time of Buddha believed that they had to experience physical suffering as the result of previous unwholesome actions. They practiced self-mortification in order to exhaust the results of unwholesome actions of past existences. When the Buddha asked them if they knew how many unwholesome acts they had committed in previous existences, they were unable to reply. The Buddha, knowing that as long as they adhered to that belief they would not be receptive to the Noble Eightfold Path, then explained to them that it was unworthy and fruitless to practice self-mortification, neither knowing if misdeeds had been committed, nor how many of them had been expiated.

Throughout India this kind of practice was widely respected as a noble undertaking long before the Buddha's enlightenment. It was universally held that only self-mortification could lead to higher knowledge, and the group of five monks also held strongly to this belief. Therefore, the Buddha began his first discourse denouncing self-mortification as too rigid. Only subsequently did he expound the doctrine of the Noble Eightfold Path.

Arduous Effort

There are some teachers whose interpretation of self-mortification contradicts the teaching of the Buddha. According to them, the earnest, tireless effort required for meditation amounts to self-mortification. The Buddha advised strenuous, unrelenting exertion and strong determination to attain the goal of concentration and insight. His own words were "Let only skin, sinew, and bone remain. Let the flesh and blood dry up. I will not stop or rest until I achieve the goal I strive for."[28] However, such strong determination only follows rigorous, unrelenting practice and effort. The ultimate aim is not immediately required of the beginner. Anything which promotes morality, concentration, and wisdom is beneficial to one's practice.

There are some who hold that contemplation on pleasant feelings constitutes indulgence in sensuous pleasure, while contemplation on painful feelings constitutes self-mortification. According to them, one should avoid both of these feelings and only contemplate on equanimity, that is, neither pleasant nor unpleasant feelings. However, in the *Mahāsatipaṭṭhāna Sutta*, the Buddha states explicitly that pleasant feeling, painful feeling, and neutral feeling are all objects for contemplation. This is reiterated in many of the other discourses. Therefore, any feeling that is experienced, whether pleasant, painful, or neutral should be observed as an object of meditation.

There are also some who say that while engaged in meditation one may repeatedly change postures in order to avoid feelings of fatigue, pain, numbness, excessive heat, or other bodily discomforts. They argue that if one persists in meditating despite unpleasant sensations, one is actually engaged in the practice of self-mortification. But meditation is an opportunity to practice patience and self-control (*khantī, saṃvara*) despite the natural processes of such bodily discomforts. One-pointedness of mind, or concentration (*ekaggatā*), can be achieved only through patiently bearing and quietly watching bodily discomfort. Continually changing postures is not conducive to the development of concentration.

The Buddha said:

> A bhikkhu meditates after making a firm resolution: "Unclinging, I will remain seated, without changing the crossed-legged position until the taints (*āsavas*) have been removed." Such a bhikkhu is an adornment to the Gosiṅga monastery in the forest of sāla trees, a valuable asset to the forest abode.[29]

Any practitioner who is not concerned with promoting sīla, samādhi, and paññā, but believes instead that suffering itself leads to nibbāna, can be considered to be practicing a form of self-mortification. Alternatively, arduous effort, no matter how painful and distressing, if undertaken for the development of sīla, samādhi, and paññā, does not constitute self-mortification.

The Buddha himself, after avoiding the two extremes (too lax or too rigid) and by following the Noble Eightfold Path, attained buddhahood and gained enlightenment.

The Benefits of Sīla, Samādhi, and Paññā

In the *Anguttara Nikāya*, the Buddha enumerated the following consolations for undertaking the cultivation of sīla, samādhi, and paññā.

> Thus, O Kālāmas, with a mind freed from greed and ill will, undefiled, and purified, the noble disciple is already during this lifetime assured of a fourfold consolation:
>
> "If there is another world, and a fruit and result of wholesome and unwholesome actions, then it may be that, at the dissolution of the body, after death, I shall be reborn in a happy realm, a heavenly world." Of this first consolation he is assured.
>
> "And if there is no other world, no fruit and result of wholesome and unwholesome actions, then I live at least here, in this world, an untroubled and happy life, free from hate and ill will." Of this second consolation he is assured.
>
> "And if evil things befall evil-doers, but I do not harbor ill will against anyone, how can I, who am doing no evil, meet with evil things?" Of this third consolation he is assured.
>
> "And if no evil things befall the evil-doer, then I know myself in both ways pure." Of this fourth consolation he is assured.[30]

VISION AND KNOWLEDGE

III. O bhikkhus, avoiding both these extremes, the Tathāgata has realized the Middle Path. It produces vision, it produces knowledge, it leads to calm, to higher knowledge, to enlightenment, to nibbāna.

With these words the Buddha informed the group of five monks that after relinquishing the two extremes he discovered the Middle Path, by means of which he attained enlightenment. The Buddha's resumption of meals after fruitless years of austerity practice enabled him to engage in meditation exercise on mindfulness breathing—an integral part of the Middle Path. As the food was taken in moderation in a mindful manner, it was not regarded as enjoyment of sensuous pleasures, nor was it self-mortification.

One who has practiced mindfulness meditation will not indulge in these two extremes. He or she will enjoy sensual objects with mindfulness; this is an example of the Middle Way without craving. Thus, there will be no indulgence in the two extremes. Furthermore, the necessary material requisites such as food, clothing, shelter, and medicine should be used with either reflective contemplation or mindfulness meditation. Whenever sense objects come into contact with mind and body, one should be aware of them as they are. Each and every moment should be noted, and one should be aware of sense objects objectively. Because of noting and objective awareness, no craving or aversion can arise. If one avoids the two extremes, one stands in the Middle Path.

Whenever sensuous objects (sight, sound, smell, taste, and touch) come into contact with the senses, seeing, hearing, smelling, tasting, and touching arise at the sense bases as the sense consciousnesses respectively. At that time, one should develop awareness in each precise moment until one realizes that objects arise and pass away and do not remain for even two consecutive moments. If at the moment of contact with one of the sense objects greed, anger, or delusion arises, these are also observed as transient objects of awareness. This realization is called insight, or "understanding things as they really are." By cultivating this understanding, one comes to have a different relationship to food, clothing, and other sense objects. One will tend not to indulge in these for the purpose of mere sensual stimulation and enjoyment. Instead, the awareness of every object appearing at the sense doors will be recognized and understood according to its true nature: as impermanent (*anicca*), suffering (*dukkha*), and insubstantial (*anatta*). Then vision will arise and the wisdom-eye will open, leading to the realization of nibbāna. When the Noble Eightfold Path is developed, the true nature of mind and matter becomes discernable. The fact of their constantly arising becomes clearly evident, as does the recognition that all these mental and material phenomena are subject to impermanence, suffering, and quiescence. In the final stage of the cultivation of the Noble Eightfold Path, the nature of nibbāna (the quiescence of all physical and mental formations and the cessation of suffering in the rounds of existence) is clearly and fully realized for oneself.

Leading to Calmness (Upasamā)

The Noble Eightfold Path leads to the calming of mental defilements (*kilesas*). For one who develops the Middle Path through awareness, concentration, and wisdom, mental defilements become reduced and calmed. However, only when one has mastered the practice can mental defilements be eradicated gradually according to the stage of insight one has attained.

Indulgence in sense pleasures or in self-mortification does not lead to the calming of defilements, but instead excites more and more of these. Once one has given in to the temptation of sensual enjoyment the craving for repeated gratification results. Coming into possession of one pleasing object leads to the desire to possess more and more. One craving brings more and more cravings. There is no end to it.

Similarly, the practice of self-mortification does not lead to calmness. One's vitality is lowered as a result of extreme austerity, and this keeps the mental defilements temporarily in check. As when one is seriously ill or suffering from painful diseases, physical strength is at a low ebb and defilements remain temporarily dormant. Once normal health and strength is regained, desires for sensual gratification make their appearance as usual. While self-mortification is practiced, gross defilements remain suppressed but subtle defilements continue to arise. For example, the defilement of wrong view of self, conceit, and even wrong belief in how to practice may still have occasion to arise.

Higher Knowledge (Abhiññā)

The Middle Path also leads to higher knowledge (*abhiññā*). The wisdom that realizes the Four Noble Truths is in this context called the higher knowledge. When one develops insight and practices the Middle Path, one understands and realizes through one's own experience the nature of the mental and material world as impermanent, suffering, and devoid of self. One sees that all the aggregates of clinging are dukkha, the suffering that one experiences as a being, an "I," or self. Due to this profound penetration into the true nature of the mental and material world, there occurs in the practitioner a sense of detachment toward all cravings and the realization that craving itself is the origin of dukkha. If one comprehends the Noble Truth of dukkha by observing any of the five aggregates of clinging, there will arise simultaneously the realization of the three remaining truths as well. This is called knowing the Four Noble Truths by means of insight, or vipassanā. As vipassanā insight attains full maturity, nibbāna is realized and the factors of the Middle Path become the noble path, in that the Four Noble Truths are known as they should be known by means of the Noble Eightfold Path. Therefore, it is said that the Middle Path gives rise to higher knowledge.

Enlightenment (Sambodha)

The Middle Path leads to enlightenment (*sambodha*) through penetrative insight (*vipassanā*). In Pāli there is no distinction drawn between the higher knowledge (abhiññā) and enlightenment (sambodha). However, abhiññā denotes vipassanā insight and the noble path insight (*ariyamaggañāṇa*) which have not yet been developed (knowledge of the path of the enlightened or noble ones of which there are four stages: *sotāpanna*, *sakadāgāmi*, *anāgāmi*, and *arahant*). Sambodha means penetrative insight through which one sees the Four Noble Truths clearly. One who has never observed mental and material objects moment to moment cannot see things clearly because ignorance (*avijjā*) obscures them. But when the noble path is developed and ignorance has been uprooted, one can see or realize things as they really are. This understanding or wisdom is called enlightenment, the realization of the Four Noble Truths.

Nibbāna

The Middle Path ultimately leads to the attainment of nibbāna. For one who penetrates the Four Noble Truths with arahant path insight and also realizes nibbāna with arahant fruit (*phala*) insight, it is the attainment of the end of suffering. Nibbāna is the final goal for those who want to be free from all forms of worldly sufferings. Therefore, it was mentioned as a separate attainment by the Buddha. If the Noble Eightfold Path is developed, the Four Noble Truths will be penetrated and nibbāna realized by arahant-magga and phala. When the arahant passes away, it is called attainment of *parinibbāna*, or final liberation. At that moment, all physical and mental phenomena cease and no further existence in the cycle of rebirth becomes possible. This is the cessation of all suffering.

Thus, one who is not involved in sense pleasures and self-mortification and practices the Middle Path that opens vision, develops knowledge, calms mental defilements, produces higher knowledge, and achieves enlightenment, finally attaining the state of nibbāna.

4

The Noble Eightfold Path

The best of paths is the Eightfold Path.
The best of truths are the four sayings.
Nonattachment is the best of states.
The best of bipeds is the seeing one.

Dhammapada, v. 273

IV. *And what is that Middle Path, O bhikkhus, that the Tathāgata has realized? It is simply the Noble Eightfold Path, namely: Right understanding, right thought, right speech, right action, right livelihood, right effort, right mindfulness, and right concentration. This is the Noble Eightfold Path realized by the Tathāgata. It produces vision, it produces knowledge, it leads to calm, to higher knowledge, to enlightenment, to nibbāna.*

THE BUDDHA'S TEACHINGS are essentially a "path of purification." The Buddha never intended that people should worship him or accept his teachings on faith alone. He wanted all beings to be free from the bondage of greed, anger, and delusion. Liberation in Buddhism means freedom from all kinds of mental impurities. In order to accomplish this, one must develop the Noble Eightfold Path. During his forty-five years as a fully enlightened one, the Buddha imparted the Dhamma according to individual capacities, aptitudes, and depths of understanding. But the essence of all the discourses recorded in Buddhist scriptures are to be found in the teachings on the Noble Eightfold Path, which are:

1. right understanding (*sammā diṭṭhi*)
2. right thought (*sammā saṅkappa*)
3. right speech (*sammā vācā*)
4. right action (*sammā kammanta*)
5. right livelihood (*sammā ājīva*)
6. right effort (*sammā vāyāma*)
7. right mindfulness (*sammā sati*)
8. right concentration (*sammā samādhi*)

The order in which the factors of the Noble Eightfold Path are listed is not to be understood as successive stages of practice. They are all to be developed together. Since each factor is linked to the others, and all are mutually supportive, the path constitutes a method of training which must be practiced as a whole in order to be effective. The above ordering of the eight factors of the Noble Eightfold Path are arranged in order of teachings (*desanākkama*). Other pedagogic approaches list the eight factors in order of arising (*uppattikkama*); in order of eradicating (*pahānakkama*); in order of practice (*paṭipattikkama*); and according to realms (*bhūmikkama*).

As we have seen, the Noble Eightfold Path comprises three aspects: moral conduct or self-discipline (sīla), concentration or mental discipline (samādhi), and wisdom (paññā). It will be helpful to understand them and explain them according to these three aspects. Right speech, right action, and right livelihood form the moral aspect. By practicing right speech, right action, and right livelihood, self-discipline is established. The meditation group is made up of right effort, right mindfulness, and right concentration. Mental discipline is established by developing these. Right understanding and right thought are aspects of wisdom. Developing these leads one to insight (vipassanā) and transcendental knowledge (*maggaphalañāṇa*), in other words, wisdom pertaining to both mundane and supramundane levels. Each of these factors of the path will be described in brief, emphasizing their practical aspects. The order of presentation will follow the order of the three trainings: sīla, samādhi, and paññā.

ONE: RIGHT SPEECH (SAMMĀ-VĀCĀ)

> What, O bhikkhus, is right speech? It is avoidance of telling lies, avoidance of slandering, avoidance of hateful or abusive language, avoidance of frivolous talk or useless chatter. Bhikkhus, avoidance of these four unwholesome speeches is called right speech.[31]

According to this definition, one should understand that religious conversation or truthfulness alone is not right speech. Abstinence from unwholesome speech is the essence of right speech. It should be noted that when occasion arises for one to speak falsely, to slander, to use abusive language, or chatter uselessly, if one restrains oneself from doing so, one is establishing the practice of right speech. Indeed, one who refrains from false speech will engage only in speech which is truthful, gentle, and beneficial and will promote harmony. The essential point is that one who abstains from wrong speech establishes the moral foundation of the path.

Furthermore, whenever one sees, hears, smells, touches, or thinks, if by awareness and insight one realizes that sense objects are impermanent, no defilements can arise that would cause the utterance of wrong speech. In this way, through mindfulness meditation, one can temporarily prevent the arising of defilements or kilesas. However, if one develops insight and attains the transcendental noble path with realization of nibbāna, then wrong speech will have been dispelled completely. As one progressively attains the stages of sainthood, one gradually uproots mental defilements which are the cause of wrong speech. It is said that the first stage of sainthood (*sotāpanna*) dispels false speech or telling lies; the third stage of sainthood (*anāgāmi*) dispels slandering and abusive language; the fourth and final stage of sainthood (*arahant*) dispels frivolous talk or useless chatter. Here speech is to be understood as any vocal action, whether following from deliberate mental intention or, if 'unthinking,' as a manifestation of a basic state of mind. If the mind is impure, one speaks wrongly; if it is pure, one speaks rightly. Therefore, purity of mind is very important.

TWO: RIGHT ACTION (SAMMĀ-KAMMANTA)

> What, O bhikkhus, is right action? It is the avoidance of killing, the avoidance of stealing, and the avoidance of sexual misconduct or misuse of the senses. O bhikkhus, avoidance of these three physical evils is called right action.[32]

Here too restraint underlies right action, whether such actions are deliberate or arise unthinkingly from mental ill-discipline. When, for instance, occasion arises for one to commit killing, stealing, and sexual misconduct, if one restrains oneself from doing them, one is establishing the practice of right action. Here physical action or kamma is based on mental volition (*cetanā*). These unwholesome deeds are committed only when the mind is overwhelmed with greed, anger, or delusion. Whenever these mental states arise in the mind, one should observe them objectively until they have disappeared or insight develops (seeing them as impermanent, productive of suffering, or insubstantial). This insight leads to the attainment of transcendental wisdom (*ariya magga*). With the development of insight meditation, mental defilements gradually fall away by themselves. The Middle Path is ultimately transcended by a state of consciousness in which all actions are spontaneously right minded. However, at the beginning, one must observe the precepts as a moral discipline and as the basis for what is to come.

THREE: RIGHT LIVELIHOOD (SAMMĀ-ĀJĪVA)

> What, O bhikkhus, is right livelihood? In this teaching, the noble disciple avoids a wrong way of living, gets his means of living by a right way. This is called right livelihood.[33]

When one's means of living is based on committing the three unwholesome physical actions and the four unwholesome vocal actions, it is called wrong livelihood. If one restrains from unwholesome actions and speech for one's means of living, it is called right livelihood.

Wrong livelihood constitutes earning one's living through unlawful or unwholesome means, such as killing and stealing. However, if one commits the three unwholesome actions and the four unwholesome types of speech outside the context of earning one's livelihood, then these constitute wrong action (*micchākammanta*) and wrong speech (*micchāvācā*) respectively, but not wrong livelihood. For instance, killing flies, mosquitoes, insects, snakes, or an enemy through anger amounts to an unwholesome act or deed, a wrong action, but not wrong livelihood. Killing animals such as poultry, pigs, goats, or fish for the market or for one's own table definitely constitutes wrong livelihood.

In general, stealing is motivated by economic reasons and is therefore called wrong livelihood. If, however, the motivation for an action is driven by revenge or habit, then it is considered wrong action and not wrong livelihood. Prostitution and the selling of arms, meat, poisons, and intoxicants are all regarded as wrong livelihood. Lying is wrong speech when not motivated by economic reasons. However, when falsehood is employed in a commercial transaction or in a court of law to promote business, it amounts to wrong livelihood.

In the beginning, one should practice right livelihood by observing the moral precepts. As one practices insight meditation positive action and right livelihood is established effortlessly.

Before one develops insight, or the noble path, it is impossible to establish these moral principles; therefore, one should take the basic five precepts (not to kill, steal, lie, commit adultery, or take intoxicants) as the foundation of practice. Monks and nuns who practice vipassanā should purify their respective precepts before practice is begun, since development of concentration and wisdom is dependent on moral purity.

FOUR: RIGHT EFFORT (SAMMĀ-VĀYĀMA)

> What, O bhikkhus, is right effort? Here in this teaching, O bhikkhus, a bhikkhu rouses his mind to avoid evil, unwholesome things not yet arisen, to overcome evil, unwholesome things already arisen, to arouse wholesome things not yet arisen, to maintain wholesome things already arisen and not to let them disappear but to bring them to growth, to maturity and to the full perfection of development. And he makes effort, puts forth his energy, exerts his mind and strives. This is called right effort.[34]

According to this teaching there are four kinds of effort:

1. There is the effort to prevent any evil or unwholesome things that have not yet arisen. One should make an effort not to do any unwholesome actions. Whenever sense objects are present, sense awareness generally arises at that moment followed by craving or aversion. If one makes an effort to develop moment to moment awareness by watching them objectively, one will be able to prevent the arising of unwholesome things or any craving or aversion.

2. There is the effort to dispel any evil or unwholesome things that have already arisen. There are three types of mental defilements: (1) the defilements that arise by committing evil physical and vocal actions (*vītikkama-kilesa*), such as killing, stealing, or lying; (2) the defilements that arise in the mind if something conditioned (*pariyuṭṭhāna-kilesa*), such as desire or anger, arises; and (3) the arising of latent dispositions, which are the result of previous unwholesome actions (*anusaya-kilesa*).

Of these three kinds of defilements, physical and vocal actions can be dispelled by practicing the moral precepts. Defilements arising in the mind can also be prevented with the practice of concentration. Latent dispositions may be calmed momentarily by insight meditation. They can be rooted out gradually only as one attains the stages of sainthood. It is with the aim of completely uprooting unwholesome latent dispositions that vipassanā meditation is practiced. One must exert great effort in meditation in order to attain the noble path which eradicates those defilements latent in the mind as subtle dispositions.

3. There is the effort to bring about pure or wholesome things which have not yet arisen. One should make an effort to accomplish any wholesome actions which have not yet been accomplished, such as acts of generosity (*dāna*), morality (*sīla*), meditation (*bhāvanā*), loving-kindness (*mettā*), compassion (*karunā*), and so on. These efforts will cultivate mental purification and the accumulation of wholesome thoughts. In short, effort should be made to introduce any type of wholesome thing which has not yet arisen. One should especially make great effort to develop awareness, concentration, and wisdom, so that one may reach the path of the noble ones.

4. There is effort to maintain the pure or wholesome states that have already arisen, and to develop them to maturity and perfection. One should make an effort to continue any meritorious deeds or wholesome things toward which there is already a disposition. One should develop objective and precise awareness at the moment of seeing, hearing, touching, feeling, thinking, or knowing sense objects. At that moment, one is not only preventing impurities or unwholesome thoughts from arising, but also endeavoring to eradicate impurities or unwholesome thoughts, speech, or action. This is perfecting insight that has already arisen. Thus, every time one is aware of each phenomenon as a meditation practice, one is developing the path of right effort.

FIVE: RIGHT MINDFULNESS (SAMMĀ-SATI)

> What, O bhikkhus, is right mindfulness? Here, in this teaching, a bhikkhu dwells contemplating the body (material qualities) in the body, ardently, clearly comprehending, and mindfully, removing covetousness and grief in the world (of corporeality); he dwells contemplating the feeling in the feelings; he dwells contemplating the consciousness in the consciousness; he dwells contemplating the mental objects in the mental objects, ardent, clearly comprehending, and mindful, removing covetousness and grief in the world (of the five aggregates). This is called right mindfulness.[35]

The path of right mindfulness is comprised of the four foundations of mindfulness—mindfulness of body, feeling, mind, and objects of the mind. Contemplation of the body (*kayānupassanā*) is carried out in either of two ways: by contemplation on respiration, ānāpāna (observing the in-breath and the out-breath) or contemplation on the thirty-two parts of the body, koṭṭhāsa (observing the separate parts of the body as head hair, body hair, nails, teeth, skin, and so on). According to tradition, one can achieve meditative absorption (*appanā-jhāna*) by these two types of meditation. Through observation of the rest of the objects of mindfulness (feeling, mind, or mental objects), one can achieve access concentration (*upacāra-samādhi*). Access concentration is suitable as a foundation for vipassanā meditation.

Anyone, therefore, who wants to develop right mindfulness should select either body, feeling, mind, or mental objects as a foundation for mindfulness or awareness. It is very important to note or to be aware of the object in the present moment. For example, if the meditator contemplates on the in-breath or out-breath, he or she must note or be aware of the precise moment of the rising or falling of the breath. While contemplating body postures—such as walking, sitting, standing, or lying down—one should be aware of each moment. If any other minor body postures are assumed, one should also become aware of these precisely and with bare attention. Another method of practice is to select the physical elements—earth, water, fire, and air—as objects of contemplation. The earth element denotes the quality of heaviness or lightness in the body; the water element refers to the quality of cohesion; the fire element refers to the quality of heat or cold; and the air element refers to the quality of motion and movement in the body. Of these, the water element, which is the quality of cohesion in the body, is so subtle that it is extremely difficult to perceive. For this reason, the elements of earth, fire, and air are recommended for mindfulness meditation.

If one experiences any feelings in the body, whether gross or subtle, one should be aware of them in the present moment. There are three kinds of feelings: pleasant, painful, and neutral (neither pleasant nor painful). Whatever the feeling experienced, one should be aware of it objectively and precisely, without reflecting upon it with discursive thought. One should not anticipate any particular feeling. One should also be aware of the state of mind in the precise moment. If there is liking or disliking, desire, anger, or doubt, these should be taken as meditation objects. When one sees, hears, smells, tastes, touches, or thinks, one should be aware of these sensations as they are. It is very important not to reject any object that arises in the consciousness; rather, accept any feeling, state of mind, or mental object as the foundation of awareness. As awareness develops, mental hindrances are overcome and access concentration arises. Then the meditator realizes that all mental and physical formations are impermanent, subject to change, and do not remain for even two consecutive moments. This realization is called insight. Thus, when awareness arises with insight or right understanding, that awareness is also known as right mindfulness.[36]

Did the Buddha Teach in Detail?

The *Dhammacakka Sutta*, as we have it today, lists the factors of the noble path only in the form of headings without any detailed elaboration of method or content. Yet, it is recounted that the Venerable Kondañña and others attained higher knowledge or became liberated by the end of the discourse. Therefore, the question arises, did they fully understand the meaning and method required in applying right mindfulness? It is certain that if they did not have a clear comprehension of the method of application, they would not have been able to develop right mindfulness. In the absence of right mindfulness, attainment of higher knowledge of the noble path and fruition is impossible.

There are two plausible explanations to this puzzle. The first is that the Venerable Kondañña and others were already fully ripe with uncommon, unique perfections (*pāramitās*), destined for final liberation upon just hearing the summary of the Noble Eightfold Path. They may have applied mindfulness upon hearing the Buddha and accordingly attained higher knowledge or a state of enlightenment. The second possibility is that when the discourse was first given, the Buddha did indeed elaborate upon the headings of the Noble Eightfold Path and expounded the four foundations of mindfulness. At the time of reciting this sutta at the First Council, however, the Noble Eightfold Path, as such and as a component of the Four Noble Truths, was condensed in the form of headings only, since there already existed separate expositions or exegeses on them in other suttas. Likewise, there are still other suttas, for example the *Satipaṭṭhāna Sutta* in the *Majjhima Nikāya*, that seem likely to have been recited in condensed form at the First Council. At the Sixth Council, held in Burma from 1954 to 1956, the missing portion of the sutta was filled in and recorded, based on the *Mahāsatipaṭṭhāna Sutta* of the *Dīgha Nikāya*. Other suttas, in addition to the *Mahāsatipaṭṭhāna Sutta*, supply expositions and elaborations on the summarized headings of the Noble Eightfold Path.

No Insight Without Mindfulness

According to Theravāda Buddhism, mindfulness and wisdom are essential for the attainment of the final goal of enlightenment. Moreover, it is considered essential that these be developed simultaneously. The Buddha taught how to cultivate mindfulness and wisdom in order to overcome human suffering and realize the Dhamma (ultimate truth). Insight wisdom in Buddhism means understanding the Dhamma through personal experience, not through reasoning or intellectual intuition. The realization of the Dhamma is not possible without developing insight and wisdom through any one of the four foundations of mindfulness (through mindfulness of body, feelings, mind, or mental objects).

At the time of the Buddha, many individuals realized the Dhamma, and became enlightened, directly upon hearing the teachings because they had fulfilled the necessary perfections (*pāramitās*) in previous existences. Their liberation became possible with only a few moments of mindfulness practice. What was essential was the practice of awareness of the objects and not just the mere fact of listening to the discourse. While right mindfulness is essential to developing the highest insight, it is not sufficient by itself. Three conditions are also necessary to achieve the goal, namely, ardor (*ātāpī*), clear comprehension (*sampajañña*), and mindfulness (*satimā*). Thus, the one who is ardent, clearly comprehending, and mindful of the object will know what causes the arising of objects and their ceasing. This is insight, knowing things as they really are (*samudaya dhammānupassī*).

SIX: RIGHT CONCENTRATION (SAMMĀ-SAMĀDHI)

What, O bhikkhus, is right concentration? Here, in this teaching, the bhikkhu, being detached from all sensual objects, detached from other unwholesome things, enters into the first stage of absorption (*jhāna*), which is accompanied by applied thought (*vitakka*) and sustained thought (*vicāra*), is filled with rapture (*pīti*) and happiness (*sukha*), born of detachment from unwholesome thoughts.

After the subsiding of applied and sustained thought, and by gaining inner tranquillity and oneness of the mind, he enters into a stage free from vitakka and vicāra, the second absorption, which is born of concentration and filled with rapture and happiness.

After the fading away of rapture, he dwells in equanimity (*upekkhā*), attentiveness, and is clearly conscious; he experiences in his person that feeling of which the noble ones say, "Happy is the man of equanimity and attentive mind" thus, he enters the third absorption.

After the giving up of pleasure and pain, and through the disappearance of previous happiness and grief, he enters into a state beyond pleasure and pain, into the fourth absorption, which is purified by equanimity and attentiveness. This is right concentration.[37]

Here, absorption, or jhāna, means not allowing the mind to wander, but to have it fixed on a single object. Jhāna is also described as that which burns out all negative forces or hindrances (*nīvaraṇa*). There are four stages of jhāna according to the suttas:

1. The first stage of jhāna is constituted by five factors, namely, vitakka (initial application); vicāra (sustained application); pīti (rapture); sukha (happiness); and ekaggatā (one-pointedness of mind).

2. After the subsiding of vitakka and vicāra through continued meditation, the second stage of jhāna arises and is constituted by the three remaining factors (pīti, sukha, and ekaggatā).

3. After the fading away of pīti through continued meditation, the third jhāna is formed with the two factors of sukha and ekaggatā.

4. In the fourth jhāna, sukha is replaced by upekkhā, so that the fourth jhāna has two factors: upekkhā and ekaggatā.

These jhānic states belong to the mundane realms known as the *rūpa* (form) and *arūpa* (formless) planes. But, if they are accompanied by the noble path and fruition consciousnesses, they then belong to the supramundane realm. Strictly speaking, only the supramundane state of concentration, or samādhi, is right concentration. However, the mundane state of concentration is also classed as right concentration if it forms the basis for the development of vipassanā meditation.

There are forty kinds of objects for the development of concentration (*samatha-bhāvanā*). The meditator can select an object that appeals most to his or her temperament. This object is called the preliminary object (*parikamma-nimitta*). One should concentrate intently on this object until one becomes so wholly absorbed in it that all thoughts are excluded from the mind. Ultimately, a stage is reached in which one is able to visualize the object even with closed eyes. On this visualized image (*uggaha-nimitta*), one concentrates continuously until it develops into a conceptualized image (*paṭibhāga-nimitta*). As one concentrates continually on this abstract object, one is said to be in possession of access concentration (*upacāra-samādhi*) and the five hindrances (*nīvaraṇas*)—namely, sense desire, hatred, sloth and torpor, restlessness and worry, and doubt—are temporarily dispelled. Eventually, one attains absorption concentration (*appanā-samādhi*), or the jhānic state.

There are three factors of the Noble Eightfold Path which are necessary for right concentration, or samādhi. First, there is the application of effort in the practice of mindfulness in order to develop moment-to-moment awareness. Second, there is the development of one-pointedness of mind, which is the ability to fix one's awareness on any object arising at the sense doors. This is a momentary concentration (as distinguished from the absorption concentration of jhānic states) because awareness is arising with different objects in different moments. Third, whatever object the mind concentrates on is perceived in terms of its ultimate reality as impermanent, unsatisfactory, and devoid of a self or an essence. These factors of samādhi together cultivate the conditions for the realization of the noble path and its fruition, nibbāna

Insight Without Jhāna

It has been argued that vipassanā can be developed only after attaining jhāna. This, it is reasoned, is on account of the capacity of the jhānas to purify the mind (*cittavisuddhi*)—a requisite for the development of insight. But this position seems extreme and dogmatic since upacāra samādhi, or access concentration, can be achieved by contemplating such objects as body postures (a practice not directed toward attaining jhānic states) while still achieving the same benefits of meditative absorption, namely, temporarily dispelling the hindrances, purifying the mind, and developing vipassanā. Many individuals have achieved arahantship with this method. The *Anussatiṭhāna Sutta* states that samādhi that is developed by the practice of the recollection of the virtues of the Buddha, for example, is adequate to be used as a basic concentration for the development of higher insight up to the state of arahantship.[38] It is very common that pīti, or rapture, can be aroused by just recollecting the virtues of the Buddha and the sangha. One who meditates on the impermanence of rapture may subsequently attain arahantship.

Furthermore, innumerable people at the time of the Buddha became liberated during the course of talks given by the Buddha, and many of these people were not skilled in jhānic practices. Nevertheless, they must have achieved purification of the mind, because their minds are said to have been sound (*kalla*), tender (*mudu*), free from hindrances (*vinīvaraṇa*), exultant (*udagga*), and gladdened (*pasanna*). At the moment the Buddha delivered the most exalted discourse of the Four Noble Truths, the audience understood and comprehended the Dhamma, attaining the highest state of insight, and becoming liberated from the bondage of greed, anger, and delusion.

Thus, definitions of right concentration given in terms of the four jhānas, or absorptions, should be regarded as an excellent method. Access concentration, although described as an inferior method, is also right concentration since it accomplishes purification of mind and the dispelling of hindrances just as the first jhāna does. It also has the same five jhānic factors. In vipassanā meditation awareness and concentration arise moment to moment with each object of mindfulness. This concentration is known as *vipassanā khaṇika samādhi,* or momentary concentration. It also has the same capacity to dispel hindrances in the same manner as access concentration. Therefore, it should be regarded both as access concentration and momentary concentration under the category of the first jhāna (as well as a weaker form of the first jhāna—meditative absorption). Jhāna means closely observing an object with strong attention. Concentrated attention given to a selected object of meditation, such as, the breath for tranquillity concentration, gives rise to samatha jhāna, whereas watching the characteristic nature of mind and body and contemplating their impermanence, unsatisfactoriness, and insubstantiality brings about vipassanā jhāna.

Threefold Concentration

There are three kinds of concentration: appanā samādhi (concentrative absorption), upacāra samādhi (access concentration), and khaṇika samādhi (momentary or vipassanā concentration). Of these, the concentration developed by meditating on a selected object until the mind absorbs onto the object is called appanā samādhi. The concentration that is able to dispel hindrances, but which has not yet reached the state of absorption, is called upacāra, neighborhood, or access concentration. Finally, the concentration developed by observing objects and their nature of arising and passing away moment to moment is called khaṇika samādhi, momentary concentration. This momentary concentration refers to the calm firm state of mind prior to access concentration. It also refers to vipassanā samādhi. Vipassanā samādhi has the same capacity to dispel hindrances in the same manner as access concentration. Therefore, it can also be called access concentration. When vipassanā concentration is well developed, the mind becomes absorbed with the object, as in concentrative absorption. This state of absorption can be experienced directly by those who practice mindfulness meditation. If momentary khaṇika samādhi arises without interruption, tranquillity is maintained and negative forces or defilements cannot arise.

SEVEN: RIGHT UNDERSTANDING (SAMMĀ DIṬṬHI)

> What, O bhikkhus, is right understanding? To understand suffering, to understand the origination of suffering, to understand extinction of suffering, to understand the path leading to the extinction of suffering; this is called right understanding.[39]

Right understanding means the realization of the Four Noble Truths, which one can realize through developing right mindfulness and right concentration. According to the commentaries (*Anguttara* and *Uparipaṇṇāsa Aṭṭhakathā*), there are altogether six kinds of right understanding:

1. right understanding of kamma as belonging to beings (*kammassakatā sammādiṭṭhi*)
2. right understanding of concentrative absorptions (*jhāna sammādiṭṭhi*)
3. right understanding of insight (*vipassanā sammādiṭṭhi*)
4. right understanding of the noble path (*magga sammādiṭṭhi*)
5. right understanding of the fruition of the noble path (*phala sammādiṭṭhi*)
6. right understanding of reobservation (*paccavekkhaṇā sammādiṭṭhi*)

In the case of understanding the fruition of the noble path and of reobservation, no specific effort is required for their development since they are realized spontaneously as a result of understanding the noble path. As soon as one attains the realization of the Four Noble Truths, realization of the four fruitions follow spontaneously. Reobservation is the reflection of the path and fruition, which also follows spontaneously after the attainment of these. Therefore, one need actively strive only for the first four kinds of right understanding.

Right Understanding of Kamma

The doctrine of kamma plays a very important part in Buddhism. It is the central point to grasp in the teachings of the Buddha, and one needs to understand it firmly before one can practice the Noble Eightfold Path. Right understanding of kamma urges the individual to understand moral causation, which includes the understanding of the ten kammically wholesome actions (*kusala kamma*)—namely, generosity, morality, meditation, reverence, service, dedication of merit, rejoicing in others' merit, hearing the doctrine, teaching the doctrine, and correcting others' wrong views. Right understanding also includes the understanding of the ten kammically unwholesome actions (*akusala kamma*)—namely, killing, stealing, sexual misconduct, lying, slandering, harsh speech, vain talk, covetousness, ill will, and wrong view. Wholesome actions bring good results. They are meritorious and lead to happiness here and hereafter. The ten wholesome actions, therefore, are called good courses of action (*kusala kammapatha*). Unwholesome actions give rise to evil consequences. They are demeritorious and lead to suffering and unhappiness here and hereafter. The ten unwholesome actions, therefore, are called evil courses of action (*akusala kammapatha*).

Kamma literally means action. The Buddha defined it as mental volition (*cetanā*). Any action one performs with pure intention is called wholesome kamma. If the intention is impure, then it is called unwholesome kamma. Kamma, therefore, is not merely the affair of external or visual deeds, but it is the motive or volition involved in thinking, speaking, or doing. Any deed devoid of will or intention cannot properly be called kamma. Therefore, moral or immoral kamma is threefold according to the doors of action—bodily action, verbal action, and mental action. Any action one performs with volition through body, speech, and mind is called kamma. Whether kamma is wholesome or unwholesome is dependent on the state of mind at the moment of the action.

The Buddha, more than once, emphatically stressed the psychological importance of kamma. "O bhikkhus, it is volition (*cetanā*) that I call kamma. Having willed, one acts through body, speech, and mind."[40] The understanding of moral causation urges a thoughtful person to refrain from unwholesome deeds and to do good. One who acknowledges moral causation knows well that it is their own actions that make their life miserable or otherwise. They know that the direct cause of the differences and inequalities of birth in this life are due to the good and unwholesome actions of past existences, as well as those of this life. Thus, they understand kamma and its results and strive to promote moral and spiritual progress. This kind of understanding, even on a mundane level, paves the way toward the realization of the Four Noble Truths.

In the endless cycle of rebirth, the law of kamma prevails with good actions leading to positive results and unwholesome actions leading to negative consequences. As a result of unwholesome kamma committed in past existences, one has to suffer ill consequences, such as , a short life span, various ailments, ugliness, poverty, and so forth. Anyone who commits an unwholesome action in this life will bear the consequences in a future existence, perhaps by being born in an inferior plane of existence and accompanied by similar painful retributions.

As a consequence of good actions performed in previous existences, one lives happily and healthily in this present life, enjoying longevity, freedom from ailments, beauty, and wealth. By refraining from unwholesome actions and performing good actions of generosity and serving others, one is reborn in higher realms of existence, enjoying the results of these good actions. By understanding the result of wholesome and unwholesome kammas, one refrains from wrongdoing and accumulates good deeds, thereby establishing morality (*sīla*), which is the foundation of concentration (*samādhi*) and wisdom (*paññā*).

The Buddha said:

> O bhikkhu, when you have purified your sīla and maintained the straight view, then, leaning on your sīla and established on it, you can develop the four foundations of mindfulness.[41]

Three Paths

Clearly, right understanding of kamma and the observance of sīla are preliminary foundations, or basic paths (*mūla magga*), that must be established before one practices meditation. As discussed earlier, on the development of vipassanā, appanā samādhi (absorption concentration) and upacāra samādhi (access concentration) are prerequisites for achieving the initial purification of the mind. Since vipassanā is a preliminary path (*pubbabhāga magga*), it needs to be developed first in order to lead to the noble path (*ariya magga*). Thus, there are three essential steps included in the Noble Eightfold Path: basic path (*mūla magga*), preliminary path (*pubbabhāga magga*), and noble path (*ariya magga*).

The Meditation Method

After fulfilling the basic requirements of understanding the law of kamma and purifying sīla, the meditator chooses one particular object on which to focus. When attention is dispersed over many objects or on some objects that are not easily observable, development of concentration will take a long time. Therefore, the meditator should limit the number of objects they are focusing on and choose a vivid object suitable to his or her temperament.

At first, the meditator may begin by contemplating their in-coming and out-going breaths. After establishing concentration for some time, the meditator should direct his or her observations not to the breath itself, but to the physical sensation of the breath. That is, one should observe the motion or movement of the breath, its heaviness or lightness, its qualities of heat or cold. To develop awareness and concentration, one should observe the entire breath in three phases, its beginning, middle, and end. For instance, when the in-breath touches the nostrils, one should be aware of its beginning, middle, and end, trying to remain with that awareness until the out-breath is felt on the nostrils. In the same way, it is necessary to be aware of the out-breath with its three phases. This awareness should also remain until the in-breath comes and touches it so there will be no gap between the two breaths. The mind will stay with the touch-feeling of the breaths, experiencing the entire breath (*sabbakāya-paṭisaṃvedī*) in each moment.

After establishing awareness and concentration by observing the physical sensation of the breath at the nostrils, the meditator can observe other mental and material objects that arise moment to moment in the body or the mind, such as seeing, hearing, smelling, tasting, touching, and thinking. The meditator should be aware of any kind of feeling that arises in the body, whether gross or subtle, painful, pleasurable, or neutral. He or she should also be aware of cravings, aversions, happiness, sorrow, grief, and all kinds of mental and physical phenomena arising in the body and mind. This should be done objectively and precisely. The meditator should not think about them until he or she has developed insight, or the understanding of the true nature of these phenomena as impermanent, suffering, and without substance or self.

According to Mahāsi Sayādaw's method, the meditator should begin by noting the element of air (*vāyo dhātu*), the characteristics of which are stiffness, pressure, and motion, and which become evident in the region of the abdomen. As the abdomen rises, note "rising." As it falls, note "falling." One begins noting just these two motions, rising and falling. But this does not comprise all that is to be done. While noting the rising and falling of the abdomen, if thinking arises, note that too as "thinking" and then return to noting the rising and falling. If some painful feeling appears in the body, note that too; when it subsides or when it has been noted for some time, return to the rising and falling. If there is bending, stretching, or moving of the limbs, the meditator must note "bending," "stretching," or "moving." Whatever bodily movement occurs, one should note it in the precise moment of its occurrence, and then return to the rising and falling of the abdomen. When the meditator sees or hears anything clearly, note "seeing" or "hearing" for a moment, and then return to the rising and falling process of the abdomen. If the meditator is aware of every process by noting it attentively, the mind becomes distinctly calm and concentrated and also realizes arising and awareness and objects differently. This is the beginning of the development of insight, which distinguishes mind from matter or object.

Vipassanā with Jhāna

The meditator who practices vipassanā after attaining jhāna is called *jhānalābhi*, or one who is accomplished with absorption. The knowledge that accompanies the jhānic concentration is *jhāna sammādiṭṭhi.* While it is not necessary for vipassanā practice, nevertheless, jhānic concentration is good in itself because it purifies the mind temporarily and is thus a good foundation for vipassanā meditation. At first, the meditator needs to attain concentrative absorption through tranquillity meditation. He or she then emerges from the jhānic state and starts to observe the jhānic factors or mental states, such as initial application, sustained application, rapture, one-pointedness of the mind, happiness, contact, volition, intention, and so forth. These mental states become very clear, as do the material states on which jhāna depends. When the meditator observes these as they arise and pass away from moment to moment, he or she realizes that in every moment all these states are impermanent, unsatisfactory, and without permanent substance. The meditator progressively attains different jhānic states, emerging from them to observe the mental and material phenomena that constitute them. As one continues to practice, vipassanā insight becomes more and more developed, leading finally to the realization of the nibbānic state. Thus the Buddha said:

> In this teaching, O bhikkhus, the bhikkhu enters and stays in the first jhāna. When he emerges from that jhānic state he contemplates on the physical body, feelings, perceptions, mental formations and consciousness that exist during the jhānic moment and he sees them as transitory, painful, and insubstantial. Seeing thus he stays with vipassanā insight so gained and attains arahanthood, the cessation of all cankers.[42]

This passage tells us how a meditator who accomplishes jhānic absorptions attains the noble path through meditating on jhānic consciousness by focusing on the mental concomitants and material qualities that have arisen and passed away in the mind-body continuum. After entering into and rising from jhānic states, the meditator who is endowed with jhānic absorptions meditates on the arising and passing away of mental and material states that occurred from moment to moment. The meditator who is not endowed with jhānas focuses on the arising and passing away of any mental and material states (for example, sensual desires, thoughts, feelings, and so on) as they occur from moment to moment until he or she realizes these to be impermanent, suffering, and insubstantial.

The Advantages of Jhāna

The meditator who is endowed with jhānas enters into a jhānic state and thus meditates on any object which is very clear. When fatigue overtakes the meditator, as a result of observing many different objects appearing at the sense doors, he or she reverts to the jhānic state to ease fatigue or relax the mind. After recuperating, one continues with the observation of mental and material objects whenever they appear. Thus based on jhāna, vipassanā insight develops until it is strong enough to lead to the realization of nibbāna through insight of the noble path (*ariyamaggañāna*).

> In these words, the Buddha talked about the time when he developed insight meditation based on jhāna. "Truly, when a meditator's samādhi and vipassanā are not yet fully mature, if he sits for a long time practicing insight meditation fatigue overwhelms him. Burning sensations fill the body as if flames are bursting out from it and sweat pours out from the armpits. The meditator feels as if hot steamy gas is rushing forth from the top of his head. The tortured mind twitches and struggles. The meditator reverts to the jhānic states to reduce the mental and physical strain and to get relief from them. In this way he refreshes himself. He then returns to the task of meditating. Sitting for long periods of time he may again fatigue himself and seek relief once more by reentering a jhānic state. Indeed, he should do so. Entering jhānic states is greatly beneficial to vipassanā meditation."[43]

The meditator who is not endowed with jhāna observes all kinds of mental and material objects. When fatigue overtakes one while meditating, one cannot, of course, seek relief by entering jhānic states. One should then revert to the limited object of the in- and out-breaths, in other words, keeping attention on the nostrils and focusing on breathing in and breathing out. By limiting the object of meditation, mental and physical fatigue and strain are alleviated. Refreshed, one can return to observation of all kinds of objects. When vipassanā samādhi becomes strengthened, the meditator is able to engage in meditation practice day and night without physical and mental discomfort or distress. At this stage, whenever objects arise, the meditator observes them objectively without effort, realizing the nature of these objects as they really are, namely, as impermanent, painful, and insubstantial. This understanding gathers speed and finally both sense objects and awareness plunge into the state of cessation. This is the realization of the state of nibbāna by means of the noble path.

The Vipassanā Path

As stated earlier, there are three stages of the Noble Eightfold Path. The basic path, which consists of the right understanding of kamma (*kammasakatā sammādiṭṭhi*) and morality (*sīla*), must first be accomplished before the start of meditation. The *samatha yānika* meditator, who has accomplished meditative absorptions before vipassanā practice, has to develop either access concentration (*upacāra samādhi*) or absorption concentration (*appanā samādhi*). The *suddha vipassanā-yānika* meditator, who practices bare vipassanā without absorption concentration, must accomplish the basic samādhi path while contemplating the four primary material elements (*mahābhūtas*). Whenever the meditator becomes aware of any sense object accompanied with one-pointedness of mind and momentary concentration (*khanika samādhi*), the mind ceases to wander to other objects. In this way, the mind becomes purified and every subsequent moment of awareness develops the vipassanā path.

The Development of Vipassanā Samādhi

Effort exerted on behalf of awareness and mindfulness of each and every sense object arising at the sense doors (feeling, seeing, hearing, thinking, and so forth) constitutes the path of right effort (*sammāvāyāma magga*). Awareness, or mindfulness, of these objects is the path of right mindfulness (*sammāsati magga*). Whenever mindfulness arises on an object and becomes fixed upon it, that is, becomes one-pointed, it is called the path of right concentration (*sammāsamādhi magga*). Together these are known as vipassanā khaṇika samādhi, or vipassanā momentary concentration. These three paths—right effort, right mindfulness, and right concentration—together make up the path of concentration (*samādhi magga*).

The Development of Vipassanā Insight

The knowledge that distinguishes sense objects from awareness arises after purity of mind has been attained through the path of concentration. This clear comprehension of the distinction between the discerning mind and the material object constitutes purification of view. For example, when the meditator observes in-breaths and out-breaths, if awareness and concentration are developed, he or she knows or distinguishes awareness from the breaths. This is followed by discernment of the nature of cause and effect while in the course of meditation. For example, the meditator may recognize that there is awareness because of in-breaths or out-breaths, that there is bending because of the desire to bend, stretching because of the desire to stretch, movement because of the desire to move. The meditator may perceive how seeing arises because there is an eye to see and an object to be seen, or that hearing arises because there is an ear to hear and a sound to be heard, and so forth.

As meditation continues the meditator becomes aware of the arising and dissolution of every object. This results in the realization of the nature of impermanence with respect to both the sense object and awareness itself. This process of the arising and passing away of mental and material states without any break leads to the conviction that saṁsāra is fearful, unpleasant, or suffering, mere insubstantiality, not responsive to one's will or control. This lucid comprehension constitutes the path of right understanding (*sammādiṭṭhi magga*).

The Buddha said "dukkhe ñānaṃ"—understanding the truth of dukkha is the path of right understanding. When one observes mental and material objects from moment to moment, one realizes the three characteristics of impermanence, suffering, and insubstantiality through one's own experience and thereby comprehends the truth of dukkha. The task of comprehending the remaining three Noble Truths can then be accomplished. (A discussion of this will follow in the section on the fourth Noble Truth, *magga sacca.*) Bending or directing the mind to comprehend the true nature of mental and material states as annicā, dukkha, and anatta is the path of right thought (*sammāsaṅkappa magga*). The two paths of right understanding and right thought are grouped together as the path of insight (*paññā magga*).

The three paths of concentration and the two paths of insight are classified as working paths (*kāraka maggas*), or task forces. They are forces for the development of awareness, concentration, and wisdom, and also for the realization of the Four Noble Truths. The path of morality (*sīla magga*)—right speech, right action, and right livelihood—has been established even before meditation begins and remains firm, becoming purer during the course of meditation. In addition to these three paths, there is a combined total of eight paths, known as preliminary paths (*pubbabhāga magga*), that are developed with the progress of vipassanā meditation.

EIGHT: RIGHT THOUGHT (SAMMĀ-SAṄKAPPA)

> What, O bhikkhus, is right thought? Thoughts free from sensuous desire (*nekkhama-saṅkappa*), thoughts free from ill will (*abyāpāda-saṅkappa*), and thoughts free from cruelty (avihimsā-saṅkappa): this is called right thought.[44]

All thoughts of good deeds are considered factors of renunciation (*nekkhama-saṅkappa*). These may include the practice of generosity, the renunciation of selfish attachments (such as going forth from home into homelessness), listening to discourses, or practicing righteousness. Practicing vipassanā meditation fulfills the thought of renunciation since it is a practice aimed at eliminating attachments and cravings. Thoughts of non-killing, wishing others well, and developing loving-kindness (*mettā bhāvanā*) render the mind free from ill will (*abyāpāda-saṅkappa*). Thoughts of non-violence, considerateness, and compassion toward other beings are thoughts free from cruelty (*avihiṃsā-saṅkappa*).

Since thoughts of killing or cruelty cannot arise during vipassanā meditation practice these two factors of right thought are fulfilled during meditation. Vipassanā meditation involves the slight bending or directing of the mind toward recognizing the reality of mental and material states in their true nature of arising and dissolving and the truth concerning their impermanence, suffering, and insubstantiality.

The basic path (*mūla magga*) and the preliminary path (*pubbabhāga magga*) are known together as the eightfold vipassanā path. When this vipassanā path becomes fully developed, it is transcended and the noble path is attained, leading to the realization of nibbāna. Therefore, the preliminary path may be called the forerunner of the noble path. In other words, they form the first and last parts of the same continuous path respectively. To attain the noble path, the meditator must first develop the vipassanā path. Having become established in the noble path, the meditator becomes a noble one and experiences the bliss of nibbāna.

5

The Four Noble Truths

Whosoever is free from sense perceptions, in him no more bonds exist;
Whosoever by insight freedom gains, all delusions cease in him;
But whosoever clings to sense perceptions and to viewpoints wrong and false
He lives wrangling in this world.

Suttanipāta, v. 159

Contemplating the rise and fall of aggregates as they really are,
I rose up with mind free (of taints); completed is the Buddha-word.

Therīgāthā, v. 96

FOLLOWING SIX YEARS OF STRUGGLE, the Buddha realized the Four Noble Truths under the Bodhi tree. These Noble Truths are found in all beings as realities of the universe. The Buddha stated:

> In this very one-fathom-long body, along with its perceptions and thoughts, do I proclaim the world, the origin of the world, the cessation of the world, and the path leading to the cessation of the world.[45]

In this particular context, the term "world" (*loka*) implies life or being. The Dhamma is an incontrovertible fact of life. Whether buddhas arise or not, these truths exist. A buddha reveals the Dhamma to the deluded world. These are called Noble Truths because they were discovered or realized by the ariyas or noble (enlightened) ones. The Buddha taught the Four Noble Truths to the five ascetics in his first sermon at Deer Park. The Four Noble Truths constitute the central tenets of Buddhism. They are:

1. The Noble Truth of suffering (*dukkha*)
2. The Noble Truth of the origin of suffering (*samudaya*)
3. The Noble Truth of the cessation of suffering (*nirodha*)
4. The Noble Truth of the path leading to the cessation of suffering (*magga*)

The Buddha is regarded as the "peerless physician" (*bhisakka*) who is capable of diagnosing exactly the illness of each and every being. It was in this manner of expression that the Buddha taught the Four Noble Truths. First, he established that the world is founded on suffering (*dukkhe loko patiṭṭhito*)[46] and that suffering is an undeniable and universal phenomenon (*pariññātabba*) one must strive to comprehend. He then established the cause of the disease: the origin of suffering is craving (*taṇhā*). Then the Buddha described the cure for the disease, which is nibbāna (*nirodha*). Finally, he recommended the remedy, which is the Noble Eightfold Path.

ONE: DUKKHA

> V. *This, O bhikkhus, is the Noble Truth of suffering (*dukkha*): Birth is suffering, aging is suffering, sickness is suffering, death is suffering, sorrow and lamentation, pain, grief, and despair are suffering, association with the unloved or unpleasant condition is suffering, separation from the beloved or pleasant condition is suffering, not to get what one wants is suffering. In brief, the five aggregates of attachment are suffering.*

Dukkha is a Pāli term that cannot be translated adequately into English. There seems to be no equivalent in any other language. In ordinary usage, the word dukkha means "suffering, pain, unsatisfactoriness, ill, sorrow, and misery," but there are further nuances. The word dukkha as it appears in the first Noble Truth represents the broadest frame of the Buddha's perspective of life and the world. It means not only ordinary suffering but also includes the deeper meaning of impermanence, imperfection, emptiness, and insubstantiality.

Threefold Dukkha

There are three aspects of the term dukkha: (1) *dukkha dukkha*, which is ordinary suffering; (2) *vipariṇāma dukkha*, which is suffering experienced by change; and (3) *saṅkhāra dukkha*, which is suffering experienced by conditioned states.

The first aspect, dukkha dukkha, contains two components of ordinary suffering. The refers to life, or being, as it is constituted by mental and material forces (*nāma-rupā*), which are known more specifically as the five aggregates (*pañcakkhandha*). The Buddha defined these five aggregates as dukkha.[47] In other words, the bare fact of life itself is dukkha. The second dukkha implies universal maladies. When mental and material forces, or the five aggregates, manifest or come into existence they are bound to be experienced as all kinds of suffering. This is the dukkha experienced in birth, old age, sickness, death, association with unloved ones and unpleasant conditions, separation from loved ones and pleasant conditions, not getting what one wants, sorrow, lamentation, pain, grief, and despair. In short, dukkha is all kinds of physical and mental suffering that are universally accepted as suffering or painful.

The second aspect of suffering is vipariṇāma dukkha. Vipariṇāma means "changing." It is the nature of the universe that things constantly change. A happy feeling, a happy condition in life—these cannot last. They are impermanent by nature. When they change, suffering, pain, or unpleasant feelings are the result. "Whatever is impermanent is suffering (*yadaniccaṃ tam pi dukkhaṃ*),"[48] said the Buddha. Whenever one is faced with worldly vicissitudes, one experiences suffering in life. These two aspects of suffering are easy to understand as they are common experiences in daily life. Because these aspects of suffering are readily recognizable as general experiences, they have typically come to stand for the meaning of dukkha referred to in the First Noble Truth. However, this does not convey the full meaning of dukkha as the Buddha used the term when referring to the First Noble Truth.

The third aspect of suffering, saṅkhāra dukkha, is conditioned states. Everything in the universe, whether physical or mental, is conditioned and conditioning. This kind of dukkha will be clearly understood through direct experience in vipassanā meditation. One who practices vipassanā needs to be aware of physical and mental phenomena until he or she realizes the ever-changing processes that constitute the universe. Then one will understand dukkha as a consequence. In order to understand this form of dukkha, the meditator focuses on the notion of a "being" or an "individual" or what is referred to as "I."

The Five Aggregates

According to Buddhism, a being or an individual, the "I," is merely a combination of ever-changing physical and mental forces or energies, which may be divided into five groups, or aggregates (*pañcakkhandha*). As stated in the *Wheel of Dhamma Discourse*: "In brief, the five aggregates of attachment are suffering." The five aggregates are:

1. The first aggregate is that of matter (*rūpakkhandha*), which includes the four great principal elements: the element of earth (*paṭhavī-dhātu*), which is the quality of heaviness and lightness in material form; the element of water (*āpo-dhātu*), which is the quality of cohesion or fluidity; the element

of fire (*tejo-dhātu*), which is the quality of heat and cold; and the element of air (*vāyo-dhātu*) which is the quality of motions and movements in the material elements. The derivatives of these four principal elements (*upādāya-rūpa*) are also included. They are the five material sense organs—the faculties of eye, ear, nose, tongue, and body—plus their corresponding objects in the external world—visible form, sound, odor, taste, and tangible things. Thus, the whole of matter, both internal and external, is included in the aggregate of matter.

2. The second aggregate is that of sensations (*vedanākkhandha*). All kinds of feelings—pleasant, unpleasant, or neutral—whether physical or mental, are experienced through the contact of physical and mental organs with the external world. All of these are included in the aggregate of sensations. There are six kinds of feelings: those experienced through the contact of the eye with visible form; ear with sound; nose with odor; tongue with taste; body with tangible objects; and the contact of the mind with mental objects, thoughts, or ideas. All our physical and mental sensations are included in this group.

3. The third aggregate is that of perception (*saññākkhandha*). Perception refers to that faculty that recognizes sensations. Perceptions, like sensations, are also of six kinds and relate to six internal faculties with six corresponding external objects. Whenever our sense organs come into contact with external objects, sensations arise and from them follows perception. It is perception that recognizes both physical and mental objects.

4. The fourth aggregate is that of mental formations (*saṅkhārakkhandha*). All volitional or mental activities are included in this group. According to the Abhidhamma, with the exception of vedanā (sensation) and sañña (perception), the remaining fifty kinds of mental activities are called saṅkhāra. These include contact (*phassa*), volition (*cetanā*), attention (*manasikāra*), will (*chanda*), determination (*adhimokkha*), confidence (*saddhā*), concentration (*samādhi*), wisdom (*paññā*), energy (*viriya*), greed (*lobha*), hatred (*dosa*), delusion (*moha*), conceit (*māna*), and so on. Saṅkhāra (mental formations) comprises all our good and bad actions and reactions in daily life. What is generally known as kamma comes under this group. The Buddha defined kamma in this way, "O monks, it is volition (*cetanā*) that I call kamma. Having willed, one acts through body, speech, and mind."[49] Volition is mental construction, mental activity. Its

function is to direct the mind in the sphere of good, bad, or neutral activities. It can, therefore, be called the stimulus for kammic formations. When our six sense faculties and their corresponding six objects in the external world come into contact, sense awareness arises. Then, respective sensations and perceptions arise. These are followed by our actions and reactions. Sensations and perceptions are not volitional actions so they do not produce any kammic force; but, saṅkhāra acts and reacts as kamma and produces kammic effects.

5. The fifth aggregate is that of consciousness (*viññānakkhandha*). Consciousness is a response, or awareness, that arises at one of the six sense faculty bases (eyes, ears, nose, and so on). For instance, visual consciousness has the eye as its base and visible form as its object. The Buddha said, "When the visible object arises at the sense eye base, visible consciousness arises (*cakkhu-viññāna*)."[50] Likewise, when sound contacts the sense ear base, odor contacts the nose base, taste contacts the tongue base, tangible things contact the body base, and mental objects contact the mind base, then hearing, smelling, tasting, touching, and mental consciousness arise at each respective sense base. Consciousness, then, is of six kinds, in relation to the six internal bases and the corresponding six external objects.

It should be noted that consciousness does not have the capacity to recognize an object as a particular thing. It is characterized only by the quality of being aware of that sense object. When the eye, for instance, comes into contact with the color blue, visible consciousness of the presence of a color arises as awareness. However, consciousness does not recognize that color as blue. There is no recognition at this stage. Perception (the third aggregate) is the faculty that recognizes and identifies the color as blue. Thus, the aggregate of consciousness is merely the awareness of sense experience arising from moment to moment at the sense bases. These sense experiences do not remain the same for even two consecutive moments, but are in a state of flux, continuously arising and vanishing.

These are, very briefly, the five aggregates. When they are combined together, we get the idea of labeling or naming them as "I" or a "being" or an "individual." However, they are all impermanent, constantly changing, and therefore they are dukkha. Thus, there is no unchanging substance, essence, or self that can be called "I" within these five aggregates or outside them. The Buddha said, "Whatever is impermanent is dukkha." Elsewhere, the Buddha expounded:

> O bhikkhus, when these five aggregates are born, decay, and die every moment, you are born, decay, and die every moment.[51]

And:

> He who sees dukkha sees the arising of dukkha, sees the cessation of dukkha, and sees the path leading to the cessation of dukkha.[52]

Therefore, one who realizes dukkha through direct experience (through meditation) fully understands the First Noble Truth of dukkha, or suffering.

TWO: THE ORIGIN OF DUKKHA

> VI. *This, O bhikkhus, is the Noble Truth of the origin of suffering: It is craving that produces rebirth, bound up with pleasure and greed. It finds delight in this and that, in other words, craving for sense pleasures, craving for existence or becoming, and craving for nonexistence or self-annihilation.*

The Buddha explained how life itself is not different from dukkha. He established that the cause of dukkha is craving, or thirst (*taṇhā*). There is no arbitrary creator who controls our destinies. Suffering and the cause of suffering are not attributable to any external agency, but can be explained by life itself. Craving, a mental factor, is the most powerful force causing not only suffering in this very life, but also the perpetuation of existence. It builds and rebuilds the world over and over again. Life depends on the desire for life. However, craving is not the first or only cause for the arising of dukkha. Craving is itself conditioned by other causes. The most immediate cause of taṇhā is vedanā, or feeling. According to Buddhism, there is no first cause. There are innumerable and beginningless causes and effects, which are interdependent and related one to the other. Things are neither due to one single cause nor are they causeless. Everything in the universe is conditioned, interdependent, and related. Craving, or taṇhā, is regarded as the proximate cause of suffering. According to the Abhidhamma, the cause of the arising of suffering, or *dukkha samudaya*, is lobha (greed), one of the fifty-two mental states. Taṇhā (also translated as "thirst"), rāga (craving), and upādāna (attachment) are closely related to lobha (greed). Lobha conditions and causes the arising of dukkha, whereas taṇhā is the root cause of suffering (*taṇhā dukkhassa mūlaṃ*).

Kamma and Rebirth

A "being" refers to the five aggregates we call a "life." Life is dukkha and dukkha is life. Taṇhā (craving or desire) is one of the mental states of a "being." When one is born as a being, one has craving or desire to be born again; and because of this desire the being accumulates wholesome or unwholesome kamma. Therefore, on a account of kamma one is born again—has another becoming (*bhava*). In other words, desire produces rebirth.

> Kamma's result proceeds from kamma,
> Result has kamma for its source,
> Future becoming springs from kamma,
> And this is how the world goes round.[53]

> For those beings who are hindered by ignorance, fettered by craving, delighting in this and that (objects), there comes to be recurrence of becoming again in the future.[54]

How Does Rebirth Take Place?

It is easy to understand that insofar as taṇhā has the nature of delighting in and clinging to objects, a being finds delight in whatever existence it is born into and enjoys any sense present there. When one wishes to remain in existence and to get or enjoy pleasurable objects, then volitional activities come into play. These kammas (volitional actions), which may be wholesome or unwholesome, are the cause of rebirth into new existences.

When a person is about to die, one of the wholesome or unwholesome kammas accumulated over the course of the person's lifetime appears at his or her sense doors. This sense object may be kamma or a sign of kamma (*kamma-nimitta*) that is, any sight, sound, smell, taste, touch, or idea that had been obtained at the time of that kamma. Alternatively, the object may be a sign of destiny (*gati-nimitta*), that is, the sign of the next existence where one is destined to take rebirth as the result of one's previous kamma. These arise with the process of consciousness for five moments just before the death moment (*maraṇāsanna-javana*) and function as a new conditioning consciousness (*abhisaṅkhāra viññāṇa*) for the rebirth.

According to the Buddha, kamma resembles a field in which consciousness may grow (*kammaṃ khettaṃ*). Consciousness is just like a seed (*viññānaṃ bījaṃ*) for the growth of the relinking consciousness (*paṭisandhi-viññāna*); and craving is likened to the moisture or water element (*taṇhā sineho*), which is an essential factor for its growth.[55] A new conditioning consciousness (*abhisaṅkhāra-viññāna*) that conditions new becoming takes as its object kamma, a sign of kamma, or a sign of destiny at the moment of dying. There are two causes for new life: kamma and taṇhā. But kamma without taṇhā cannot bring about new becoming. Taṇhā is the main cause. Therefore, it is said that taṇhā produces rebirth.

The consciousness that arises at the first moment of conception, known as relinking consciousness, also takes as its object kamma, a sign of kamma, or a sign of destiny. The relinking consciousness is followed by the life continuum consciousness (*bhavaṅga citta*), which goes on continuously throughout life, even if there is no sense consciousness arising. According to the Abhidhamma, relinking consciousness, life continuum consciousness, and death consciousness within a single life are all in the same category. They arise as the result of one particular kamma in the past life that appeared at the moment of dying. Thus, taṇhā forms the root cause of the new existence or new becoming.

Craving for Sense Pleasure

When we experience any kind of suffering or pain in this life, it is because of our craving for or attachment to sense objects. For instance, if our child is ill, we are worried and feel lots of suffering. But if another person's child is ill, we don't worry or feel as much, because we don't have so much attachment to another's child. Anything that we have attachment to or craving for, which changes or is lost, causes suffering. The Buddha said:

> From craving arises grief, from craving arises fear;
> for he who is free from craving there is no grief, much less fear.[56]

Greed, desire, thirst, lust, yearning, and affection are some of the characteristics included in the term craving. Craving is the enemy of the whole world; it is through craving that all unwholesome things come to living beings. Craving and attachment can arise for physical and non-physical things. Thus, we can have craving for and attachment to sense objects, wealth, or property as well as to rites and rituals, philosophy, views, ideas, or religion, all of which can lead to suffering, frustration, and unsatisfactoriness.

Now, where and how does this craving arise or take place? Where there is delight and attachment (*nandī-rāga sahagatā*), craving arises and manifests.

All sixfold sense bases are the place at which craving arises, because it is through these bases that a person recognizes sense objects. When one sees an object, then one reacts with like or dislike. Likewise when one hears sound, smells, tastes, touches, and thinks, then like or dislike arises. Some may say that there is no difficulty in accepting liking as craving, but how can one accept that disliking is craving, for it is aversion or hatred. On saying that if one dislikes a particular thing it means one likes something else. Therefore, both like and dislike are regarded as craving. Visual forms, sounds, smells, tastes, tangible things, and thoughts or ideas are delightful and pleasurable and when these objects arise at their respective sense organs, craving arises. The craving that arises with regard to sense objects is called kāma-taṇhā, or sensual craving.

Craving for Becoming

Craving associated with belief in eternal existence, is called "craving for existence or becoming" (*bhava-taṇhā*). When sensual objects arise, one develops craving as like or dislike, and according to one or the other, one accumulates wholesome or unwholesome kamma as a result of which one has to be reborn again. There are some people who believe in a future life and crave to be born again in a better life. Therefore, they attempt to accumulate good kamma so that they may be reborn into a better life. However, this is also a form of dukkha, for "birth is also suffering" (*jāti pi dukkhā*). Craving for becoming, the desire to continue existing, or to continue to be reborn forever is what is known as the view of eternalism (*sassata-diṭṭhi*).

Craving for Annihilation

When craving is associated with the belief in self-annihilation, it is called craving for nonexistence (*vibhava-taṇhā*). This is what is known as the view of nihilism (*uccheda-diṭṭhi*). Believing there are no consequences to his or her actions, the nihilist may reject all religious moral principles, as well as the belief in life after death or future existences. Such a person may perform moral or immoral actions. But irrespective of the rejection of the consequences, whether one believes in kamma or not, the result of kamma will be that one is born again into existence. To be born again is dukkha. As long as one remains in the cycle of rebirth, or saṁsāra, there is dukkha, regardless of whether the rebirth is happy or unhappy. Therefore, it is said that these three kinds of taṇhā are the origin, or root cause, of suffering.

THREE: THE CESSATION OF DUKKHA

VII. This, O bhikkhus, is the Noble Truth of the cessation of suffering. It is the complete cessation of suffering; giving up, renouncing, relinquishing, detaching from craving.

The cessation of suffering (*nirodha*) is known as nibbāna, which literally means "freedom from craving." While the literal meaning may help one to understand the term, it can not help one to experience the bliss of nibbāna. Only the one who applies the Noble Eightfold Path of sīla, samādhi, and paññā can comprehend the full meaning of nibbāna through direct experience. It is impossible to make one understand with mere explanations or definitions. Just as the sweetness of mango fruit cannot be made known to one who has no previous experience of it until he puts a small piece on his tongue, so too must one "taste" nibbāna.

Nibbāna is the *summum bonum* of Buddhism. Although many terms are used to describe it and many detailed explanations provided, the actual understanding of nibbāna remains elusive to those who would only seek to comprehend it analytically and conceptually (*atakkāvacaro*). The Buddha defined nibbāna in both positive and negative terms. But, nibbāna is neither positive nor negative, for the idea of both negative and positive are relative and dualistic, whereas nibbāna is absolute reality and beyond duality and relativity. These terms cannot fully express the true meaning of nibbāna, which can only be realized through meditation and mental training. For those who delight in sensual pleasures it is difficult to imagine what a blissful and sublime state might be like which is not characterized by any of the qualities experienced through the five sense doors.

Nevertheless, if nibbāna is described and defined in positive and negative terms, one may still get some notion about what nibbāna means in relative language. In this discourse, the Buddha used the word *dukkha-nirodha* (cessation of dukkha). Although the word nibbāna is not mentioned, these words are synonymous. In positive terms, nibbāna means peace (*santi*), sublimity (*paṇīta*), purity (*suddhi*), release (*vimutti*), security (*khema*), excellent happiness (*paramasukha*), and so forth; while in negative terms it is defined as deathless (*amataṃ*), unconditioned (*asaṅkhata*), extinction of craving (*taṇhākkhayo*), extinction of hatred (*dosakkhayo*), extinction of delusion (*mohakkhayo*), cessation of dukkha (*nirodha*), extinction of thirst (*virāga*), and so on.

Saupādisesa Nibbāna

There are two kinds of nibbāna: *saupādisesa-nibbāna*, meaning "nibbāna with the aggregates remaining" and *anupādisesa-nibbāna*, meaning "nibbāna without the aggregates remaining." The meditator who practices vipassanā meditation attains stages of insight and subsequently enters the stream of the noble path. At that time, he or she realizes for the first time the bliss of nibbāna. During vipassanā meditation the meditator realizes that the whole of mentality and materiality, which is held as "I," or a being, is impermanent (anicca), suffering (dukkha), and insubstantial (anatta). As the meditator's understanding and awareness develops to its culmination, awareness suddenly ceases. He or she sees the other side of reality (the realization of the cessation of dukkha). This is the first moment in which the meditator experiences the bliss of nibbāna in his or her beginningless round of saṁsāra. Such a person is called a sotāpanna, or stream winner—the one who can reobserve the bliss of nibbāna as fruition (phala). This nibbāna is called "nibbāna with the aggregates remaining."

Likewise, those who practice with the aim of reaching higher stages uproot defilements according to the stages reached in the holy life. Their experience is also of nibbāna with a base (substratum) remaining. The arahant, one whose taints (*āsava*) are completely destroyed through the practice of meditation, experiences the bliss of nibbāna. This kind of nibbāna is called "nibbāna with a base remaining." Although the arahant is liberated from the bonds of becoming, such as, greed, anger, and delusion, his sense faculties have not yet been demolished and he experiences pleasure and pain, because his five aggregates still remain. The extinction of greed, hatred, and delusion describes "nibbāna with a base remaining" (*saupadisesa nibbāna dhātu*). When the Venerable Sāriputta, the chief disciple of the Buddha, was asked by the devotee Jabukhādaka, "Nibbāna, nibbāna, is the saying, friend, Sāriputta. What is nibbāna?" Sāriputta replied, "the destruction of lust, the destruction of hatred, the destruction of delusion, friend, is called nibbāna."[57] It is also called the cessation of defilements (*kilesa-nibbāna*). Therefore, it is said, in Theravāda Buddhism, that it is possible to experience the bliss of nibbāna here and now, in this very life. There is no need to wait until you die.

Parinibbāna

There are three rounds of becoming: kamma, defilements or kilesa, and the results of kamma or vipāka. These are interdependent, repeatedly coming into existence as the wheel of life, or saṁsāra. When one is born as a being (becoming), this is the birth of the five aggregates. Whenever sense objects arise at the sense bases, craving and attachment motivated by ignorance arise. Thus, by craving sense objects one accumulates wholesome and unwholesome kamma. Then, as a result of kamma, one has to be born again. However, for the arahant who totally eradicates all traces of defilements that lead to becoming or rebirth, there is no more rebirth. He is liberated from the cycle of saṁsāra, from repeated existence. The arahant may have performed many good deeds in his lifetime, but his actions are ineffective for they are not motivated by mental defilements (kilesa) such as greed (lobha), hatred (dosa), and ignorance (moha). Any action that gives a result is called kamma. The action that does not give any wholesome or unwholesome result is called *kiriya* (functioning). A seed cannot grow without soil and fertilizer. Likewise, for the arahant who has uprooted ignorance and desire, there is no fertile soil in which kammic energies can arise and produce a result. When the arahant dies, the five aggregates cease. When the wax and wick of a candle burn down, the flame dies out. In the same way, the arahant who has no kamma will upon death have no further becoming. There is only the end of dukkha—peace. This is "nibbāna without the aggregates remaining" and is known as parinibbāna, or the final passing away of the arahant.

> There is, O bhikkhus, the unborn, unoriginated, unmade, and unconditioned. Were there not the unborn, unoriginated, unmade, and unconditioned, there could be no escape for the born, originated, made, and conditioned. Since there is the unborn, unoriginated, unmade, and unconditioned, there is escape for the born, originated, made, and conditioned.[58]

Because nibbāna is expressed in negative terms, some may think that it is negative and expresses self-annihilation. Nibbāna is not annihilation of self, because there is no self to annihilate. Rather, nibbāna can be said to be the annihilation of craving, hatred, delusion, and the false perception of selfhood. Nibbāna does not signify nothingness. Nibbāna is ultimate truth or reality, incomprehensible to the experience of the worldly person. It is the domain of saints only, and is realized by the wisdom of their own experience (*paccattaṃ veditabbo viññūhi*).

FOUR: THE PATH LEADING TO THE CESSATION OF DUKKHA

> *VIII. This, O bhikkhus, is the Noble Truth of the path leading to the cessation of suffering. It is simply the Noble Eightfold Path, namely: Right understanding, right thought, right speech, right action, right livelihood, right effort, right awareness, and right concentration.*

Because the noble path has already been elaborated upon, only the points necessary for an understanding of how to practice the Middle Way will be discussed again. The Noble Eightfold Path is comprised of three aspects: sīla, samādhi, and paññā. These three aspects are the conditions for eradicating the three kinds of defilements, or kilesa: (1) mental defilements that arise by transgression of ethical precepts (*vitikkama- kilesa*); (2) mental obsessions that arise due to conditions (*pariyuṭṭhāna- kilesa*); and (3) latent tendencies or dispositions (*anusaya-kilesa*).

If one observes sīla—which is comprised of right speech, right action, and right livelihood—one will not cultivate unwholesome actions, such as, harming living beings, stealing, sexual misconduct, and wrong speech. If one practices samādhi—which is comprised of right effort, right awareness, and right concentration—then mental obsessions or any reaction of like and dislike will not arise whenever sense bases come into contact with sense objects. For those who practice samādhi, like or dislike does not arise, because when they see or hear they are aware of these just as seeing and hearing. Latent tendencies are those mental defilements that are stored in the mind as dispositions in the beginningless cycle of rebirth as a result of unwholesome actions. These kinds of subtle defilements can be uprooted through paññā, which is constituted by right understanding and right thought. The main root cause of these dispositions is avijjā, or ignorance. Avijjā is delusion or darkness, and paññā is wisdom or light. When light arises, the darkness disappears; when one's mind is free from delusion, it is in the state of enlightenment. Therefore, the Buddha instructed on three kinds of training to purify the three kinds of impurities of the mind.

The eight paths and the three aspects of training should be practiced simultaneously, not in numerical order. When one experiences problems or unpleasant feelings, it is because of one's own mind: one sees or hears and gives judgement, positive or negative, according to one's own disposition. For example, one sees something for the first time and likes what one sees and is happy, but on seeing it for the second time does not like it and is unhappy; the feeling of unhappiness is not because of the thing itself, but on account of the change in one's attitude or state of mind. "Because the mind is defiled, beings suffer (*cittasaṃkilesā sattā saṃkilissanti*),"[59] said the Buddha. We are responsible for our own happiness and sorrow. We create our own heaven and hell. Our judgments and feelings are dependent on our own ego, or personality, and the ignorance that is latent in the mind. The aim of the teaching of the noble path is to purify the mind.

Higher Morality

Before practicing samādhi and paññā, it is essential to establish sīla by observing the five moral precepts (*pañcasīla*), or code of discipline. If, however, the aim of practice is to achieve the highest wisdom or enlightenment, then the higher morality (*adhisīla*) is required. This is because unwholesome actions and speech are performed only when the mind is overwhelmed by greed, anger, or delusion. Kamma is mental volition and not the function or manifestation of the action. According to the state of mind at the time of action, kamma (volition) becomes wholesome or unwholesome. The meditator who does not practice other aspects of samādhi and paññā is unable to achieve higher morality. As one develops samādhi and paññā, so the quality of morality is also developed. It is very common to find that worldly persons are able to observe morality whenever the situation is positive or good. If, however, the situation is negative or unsuitable, they find it much more difficult to observe moral precepts. There are many people who practice meditation regularly, live in the community with harmony, and talk about patience and compassion, but find it difficult to live with others outside of the community. As mentioned before, there are mental obsessions that arise only when a situation is changed. If one does not uproot latent mental aberrations or defilements, when the situation is unsuitable or against one's own ideal, the reaction of like and dislike, or craving and aversion, arises. These become mental obsessions and negative forces of the mind conditioning the accumulation of unwholesome actions. Through the practice of vipassanā, unwholesome mental dispositions become eradicated, thereby developing the practitioner's sīla, which itself becomes a precondition to higher wisdom.

The list of the Noble Eightfold Path is headed by right understanding. Right understanding (*sammā diṭṭhi*) means knowing things as they really are. The Buddha said, "Right understanding is to understand suffering, to understand the cause of suffering, to understand the cessation of suffering, and to understand the path leading to the cessation of suffering." The wisdom that realizes the truth of suffering is right understanding. Right understanding is so essential to the path that the Buddha taught it first.

The Noble Eightfold Path is intended not merely as an intellectual exercise, but as a practical undertaking. If one understands the nature of dukkha, one realizes all Four Truths as well. To understand dukkha is essential, which is why the list of the Eightfold Path is headed by right understanding. Those who understand the truth of life as suffering are able to practice vipassanā, which leads to the attainment of nibbāna. The order in which the eight paths are listed in the Noble Eightfold Path is not significant in the sense that each path requires completion before moving on to the next one. All eight paths are interdependent and interrelated, and at the highest level function simultaneously. At the beginning of practice, each path needs to be infused with some degree of right understanding, for it is the pillar of the teachings.

> O bhikkhus, it is through not understanding, not penetrating the Four Noble Truths, that we have run so long, wandered so long in this round of existence (saṁsāra) both you and I. When these Four Noble Truths, O bhikkhus, are understood and penetrated, rooted out is the craving for existence (bhava-taṇhā), destroyed is that which leads to renewed becoming, and there is no more coming to be.[60]

By right understanding alone, one cannot realize the true nature of anicca, dukkha, and anatta. Right thought is also required. Right thought includes thoughts of selfless renunciation, love, and non-violence extended toward all living beings. It is a pure and balanced state of mind without which right understanding cannot be developed. The meditator must investigate the true nature of the physical and mental worlds from moment to moment in order to understand them as they really are. For this reason, the Buddha taught right thought after he taught right understanding.

Meditation on the Four Noble Truths

Although meditation on the Four Noble Truths is noted in the *Mahāsatipaṭṭhāna Sutta*, only two of these truths, dukkha and the origin of dukkha, are considered suitable for the practice of meditation. These two truths are mundane while the other two are supramundane. Meditation requires observation of objects that are mundane and conditioned. Supramundane states are not suitable for meditation because they are beyond the grasp of ordinary worldlings. They cannot have the noble path and fruition (*magga-phala*) as an object of meditation before attaining *gotrabhu*, which is the state of consciousness that has realized nibbāna and that changes one's lineage from a worldling to a noble one.

When vipassanā insight becomes fully developed, adaptable insight (*anuloma-ñāna*) arises, which is followed by gotrabhu insight. Following immediately after gotrabhu is the realization of the noble path and fruition. At the moment of gotrabhu, the meditator experiences a glimpse of nibbāna. Before that moment, it is not possible to take nibbāna as the object of meditation, nor the paths and fruitions. However, those who practice contemplation on the attributive qualities of nibbāna (*upasamānussati*), such as being devoid of lust (*virāga*), can gain tranquillity or concentrative absorptions. But this practice is taken solely for the purpose of achieving one-pointedness of mind and not the realization of the Four Noble Truths.

The meditator should take the five aggregates as a meditation object. If the meditator observes one of the five aggregates with awareness, and realizes the truth of dukkha, that moment of penetrative insight (*paṭiveda*) permits a simultaneous understanding of the other three truths as well. At the time of awakening (*abhisamaya*) the meditator comprehends that suffering is to be rightly understood, that the cause of suffering (*taṇhā*) is to be abandoned, that the cessation of suffering (*dukkhanirodha* or *nibbāna*) is to be realized, and that the path leading to the cessation of suffering (*dukkhanirodhagāmini paṭipadā*) is to be developed. Indeed, through the development of the Noble Eightfold Path the meditator comprehends life, which is the five aggregates, as dukkha; eradicates the origin of dukkha (*taṇhā*); and experiences the bliss of the cessation of suffering (*nirodha*), which is the realization of nibbāna.

When one practices vipassanā, the object of meditation must be one of the five aggregates or mental and material (*nāma-rūpa*) elements. The meditator should observe the object until it is clearly understood as impermanent. This leads to the comprehension that because all things are impermanent they are dukkha and also devoid of self. When the meditator comprehends these characteristics of dukkha, anicca, and anatta through the direct experience of them as universal laws, he or she has then realized the Four Noble Truths. He or she becomes an ariya, a noble one.

6

The Seven Stages of Purification

When a wise man established well in virtue
Develops consciousness and understanding;
Then as a bhikkhu ardent and sagacious,
He succeeds in disentangling this tangle.

Saṃyutta Nikāya, 1.13

THE MAIN AIM OF FOLLOWING the Noble Eightfold Path is to attain the state of enlightenment, the realization of nibbāna. The path to enlightenment must develop through the seven stages of purification with their corresponding levels of insight. The meditator can ascertain his or her own level of progress according to the level of insight experienced. These stages of insight are as follows.

One: Purity of Morality (Sīla-Visuddhi)

Right speech, right action, and right livelihood are basic practices for moral purification. Traditionally, observance of either five or eight moral precepts is considered adequate for the lay person striving to achieve the moral purity necessary to undertake vipassanā meditation. For monks and nuns, additional precepts are observed according to the disciplinary monastic rules (*patimokkhasaṃvara sīla*). The morality of restraining the senses (*indriyasaṃvara sīla*), the morality of pure livelihood (*ājīvapārisuddhi sīla*), and the morality of the proper use of requisites (*paccayasannissita sīla*) are essential precepts required by the meditator in order to control the senses for higher morality and to discipline the mind.

Two: Purity of Mind (Citta-Visuddhi)

When one first begins meditation, one finds it very difficult to control the mind and to concentrate on an object. The mind wanders and thoughts frequently arise because the mind is not yet fully purified. The meditator feels there is no progress in the practice. In order to progress, the meditator must achieve purity of mind by developing one of the three concentrations:

momentary concentration, access concentration, or absorption concentrations. Right effort, right awareness, and right concentration are grouped together as "concentration" (samādhi) in the Noble Eightfold Path. These three factors must be developed to purify the mind, which is otherwise perpetually inclined toward sense objects. Once a sense object arises in the senses, one reacts with like or dislike. This brings about thoughts that cause the arising of impurities. Sometimes there may be no like or dislike and no defilements, but there are interruptions that become hindrances to the practice. One should develop concentration to purify the mind. For the meditator who practices vipassanā meditation with momentary concentration (*khaṇika samādhi*), awareness arises objectively and precisely on many different successive objects. At this level, there is no reflexive thinking about the object. There is only bare awareness as the mind concentrates upon the object. When the mind becomes free from mental hindrances and awareness arises uninterruptedly with its respective objects, then concentration is established along with purity of mind. The development of vipassanā insight may then progress.

THREE: PURITY OF VIEW (DIṬṬHI VISUDDHI)

Purification of view generally denotes the overcoming of the false idea of self, or essence, in the so-called being. The meditator endowed with purity of mind observes mental and material processes in each moment, understanding the mind and body analytically. While concentrating on breathing, he or she comes to distinguish between the in-breath and the out-breath and becomes aware that the interval between the in-breath and its awareness and the out-breath and its awareness arise as different processes. In this way, the meditator comes to recognize through direct experience that each mental and material state is a different process. The same logic applies in the case of the other sense functions. For example, when seeing a visual object, one knows to distinguish each single factor involved in the process. The eye, the visual object, seeing, and awareness are all perceived as distinct factors in the visual process. By observing each of these, the meditator can analyze mental and material states according to their true essential nature. This is called "analytical knowledge of mind and body" (*nāma-rūpa pariccheda ñāna*). When this knowledge has come to maturity, the meditator understands that there is no essential unchanging self, or essence, in any mental or material process. This is called purification of view.

> No doer of the deeds is found, no being that may reap their fruits;
> Empty phenomena roll on, this is the only right view.[61]

FOUR: PURITY BY OVERCOMING DOUBT (KAṄKHĀVITARAṆA VISUDDHI)

"Purity by overcoming doubt" is that knowledge that comes about through comprehending the conditions for the arising of mental and physical phenomena. One overcomes doubts such as: "Have I been in the past? Shall I be in the future? Am I now? Am I not?" The understanding of dependent origination, of kamma, and rebirth are also included here.

> Who wishes to escape from doubt, should be attentive and alert;
> And should of mind and body both, perceive the cause and origin.[62]

As the meditator's concentration and knowledge develops, he or she realizes cause and effect while observing mind and body. When changing the sitting position, the meditator realizes that there is an intention that precedes the act. When stretching a limb, there is first the intention to stretch a limb. The meditator distinguishes between cause and effect in each moment. This is the insight that distinguishes between cause and effect (*paccaya-pariggaha ñāna*).

As time passes, the meditator comes to experience various painful feelings in the body. Just as awareness of one feeling arises, another arises somewhere else. The meditator follows each feeling as it arises and becomes aware of it. But although he or she is engaged in watching these feelings as they arise, only their initial phase of 'arising' is perceived and not their final phase of dissolution. Similarly, as mental images arise the act of awareness is noticed, but not of their moment of dissolution. In this way, the meditator understands and realizes that all mental and material processes are conditioned or conditioning. Apart from these, there is no person or self who performs or governs this phenomenal world. This is called the purity of insight by overcoming doubt.

FIVE: PURITY BY INSIGHT AND VISION OF WHAT IS PATH AND NOT PATH (MAGGĀMAGGAÑĀNADASSANA VISUDDHI)

As the meditator continues the meditation with perfect awareness and concentration, he or she becomes aware that every process of the mind and body being observed is subject to change. The processes are impermanent, just arising and passing away. Such knowledge is called the insight that observes, explores, and grasps impermanence (*anicca sammassana ñāna*).

Recognizing all mental and physical phenomena as impermanent, the meditator realizes that they are not worth cherishing. The meditator considers them as a form of suffering (*dukkha sammassana ñāna*). He or she comprehends that they are absent of self, as the processes of impersonal phenomena (*anattanupassanā ñāna*). The comprehension that arises with direct experience is called "insight by comprehension of phenomena" (*sammassana ñāna*).

As the meditator brings attention to bear on any process of the mind or body, the arising and dissolution of each process becomes prominent. This is the insight of arising and passing away (*udayabbaya ñāna*). As the meditator observes all mental and material processes objectively in the moment, as a result of insight, various phenomena arise in him or her. These may include: a brilliant light, strong mindfulness, strong or lucid awareness, strong faith, rapture, tranquillity of mind, sublime happiness suffusing the body, vigor, equanimity, but also a liking or subtle attachment to these. The meditator, at first, is delighted with these experiences believing he or she has attained the goal. However, observing these objectively, the meditator realizes they are mere phenomena, subject to change and therefore corruptions of insight. This understanding is called, "purity by knowledge and vision of what is path and not path.

SIX: PURITY BY KNOWLEDGE AND VISION OF THE COURSE OF PRACTICE (PAṬIPADĀÑĀNA DASSANA VISUDDHI)

As the meditator continues practice, the watching of arising and passing away becomes accurate and mature, keen and strong. The meditator perceives only two factors in each moment—object and awareness. While giving attention to these, he or she becomes aware that every factor is dissolving. For instance, when hearing, seeing, smelling, or thinking, dissolution and not arising becomes prominent. This is the arising of the insight of dissolution (*bhaṅga ñāna*). With the development of the insight of dissolution, awareness of fear arises in the wake of the constant and rapid dissolution of all processes. This is insight with the awareness of fearfulness (*bhaya ñāna*). Perceiving the rapid dissolution of all psycho-physical phenomena, the meditator sees them as undesirable and harmful. This is the insight of misery (*ādinava ñāna*). Psycho-physical manifestation is regarded as insubstantial, devoid of pleasure, and tiresome. This is the insight of disgust (*nibbidā ñāna*). These latter three insights are combined together as a single insight. Therefore, some meditators may experience only one or two of these.

As the meditator experiences all the processes of mind and body—fearfulness, misery, and disgust—a desire arises to renounce this mind-body complex. This is the insight of desire for deliverance (*muñcitukamyatā ñāna*). The meditator makes a strong determination and effort to develop awareness and concentration. All the processes of physical and mental elements become calm and balanced. Painful feelings disappear. Awareness arises smoothly and spontaneously, and equanimity continues for a longer time than previously experienced. This is the insight of "equanimity of formations" (*saṅkharupekkhā ñāna*).

With the maturing of this insight, awareness becomes sharp, occurring two or three times rapidly and without any special effort. This last stage is called insight leading to emergence (*viṭṭhāna gāmini*), or insight of adaptation (*anuloma ñāna*). Vitthāna means the noble path that ascends to and glimpses nibbāna. Gāmini means the special insight that proceeds to the noble path. Anuloma ñāna is the last of the vipassanā insights that occur in the progression of vipassanā insights and the noble path. If the meditator experiences this last vipassanā insight, it is called purity by insight and vision in the course of practice. Immediately afterwards, a kind of insight arises that falls, as it were, for the first time into nibbāna, which is void of formations since it is the cessation of them. This is called maturity insight (*gotrabhu ñāna*). Gotrabhu literally means "the one who has become of the lineage." In other words, by attaining that insight, one moves from the worldling lineage to that of the noble ones.

Seven: Purity by Insight and Vision (Ñānadassana Visuddhi)

The moment of the arising of path insight (*magga-ñāna*) is called purity by insight and vision, the last of the seven purifications. After the insight of adaptation (*anuloma ñāna*), maturity insight, and path and fruition insights follow in succession. The path insight lasts only for a fleeting moment and realizes the cessation of all processes of conditioning. The insight of fruition is followed by two or three insights of retrospection (*paccavekkhaṇa ñāna*) that contemplate the path of vipassanā, and the path of the noble ones. Path insight (which signifies purity by insight and vision) and fruition insight are insights of a stream winner (*sotāpanna*). The stream winner is one who enters for the first time the stream of the noble path, thereby overcoming the concept of an everlasting self, doubts about the path or teachings, and adherence to wrong rites and rituals. The stream winner has become free from rebirth in any of the lower realms of existence.

The individual who wishes to attain higher insights and stages of enlightenment should make an effort to develop vipassanā insights beginning with the insight of arising and dissolution (*udayabbaya ñāna*). This will lead to higher paths and fruition insights through which one eradicates the remaining fetters of defilements. The final stage arrived at is that of the arahant. For the arahant there can be no further rounds of rebirth in saṁsāra.

PROFOUND KNOWLEDGE (PARIÑÑĀ)

For one practicing vipassanā meditation, in order to attain the noble path, it is necessary to develop three kinds of profound knowledge in the progress of meditation stages: (1) full understanding as the known (*ñāta-pariññā*); (2) full understanding as investigating or judging (*tiraṇa-pariññā*); and (3) full understanding as abandoning (*pahāna-pariññā*). These are explained as follows.

1. When one observes physical and mental processes with awareness and concentration, they are seen precisely, from moment to moment, without concepts. For example, if a visible object arises at the eye base, it is recognized only as seeing (not as a tree or chair, and so on). In the next moment, if a sound is heard it is recognized only as hearing (not as clap, voice, and so forth). Thoughts arise and are known only as thinking. If attention is focused on the body, the quality of heaviness, lightness, heat, cold, or motion is noticed. In this way, the meditator discerns mental and material phenomena in their true nature. This is called full understanding as the known (*ñāta pariññā*).

2. If the meditator observes whatever mental and material processes arise in the body or mind objectively, he or she realizes their true nature (*tathatā*) as impermanent, suffering, and void of a permanent self or soul. There are two kinds of impermanence, radical change (*aññathābhāva*) and subsequent change (*vipariṇāma*). A change from one stage to another, or one situation to another, is radical change, while moment-to-moment changing is subsequent change. The meditator realizes that every phenomenon is an ever-changing process. There is no moment, no instant, when the changing stops. All phenomena are seen as suffering and clearly understood as devoid of soul or self. In other words, the meditator sees anicca, dukkha, and anatta. This profound knowledge is called full understanding as investigating (*tiraṇa pariññā*).

3. When the meditator's understanding of the three characteristics of all physical and mental phenomena becomes profound, there then develops a full understanding that enables him or her to dispel hallucinations (*vipallāsa*), or erroneous observations; that is, taking that which is true as being false, and that which is false as true. There are three kinds of hallucination: hallucinations of perception, thought, and view. One erroneously perceives, thinks, and views impermanence as permanence, impurity as purity, suffering as happiness, and soullessness as soul. If the meditator perfectly discerns the true nature of the phenomenal world, these hallucinations become dispelled.

The Threefold Path

The basic path (*mūla magga*), preliminary path (p*ubbabhāga magga*), and noble path (*ariya magga*) have already been explained in reference to the realization of the Four Noble Truths, or attainment of enlightenment. The basic path includes the right understanding of kamma, the establishment of morality, and the accomplishment of concentration. The meditator should accomplish one of three following kinds of concentration before the practice of vipassanā insight meditation: absorption concentration (*appanā samādhi*), access concentration (*upacāra samādhi*), and momentary concentration (*vipassanā khaṇika samādhi*). The concentrated mind dispels the hindrances, so that purification of mind may be achieved. This basic path is an essential part of the practice.

VIPASSANĀ, THE PRELIMINARY PATH

Vipassanā practice is the application of the Noble Eightfold Path, but it is only the preliminary path before the meditator enters into the stream of the noble path. After establishing the basic path, the meditator practices vipassanā by observing physical and mental processes within the five aggregates of attachment, which are misunderstood as a self or being.

As the meditator develops awareness and concentration, his or her understanding or insight develops and he or she realizes these processes as they really are. The meditator experiences the insight stages accordingly. Whenever the meditator is engaged in meditation, there are five factors of the Eightfold Path present; three from the concentration group (right effort, right awareness, and right concentration) and two from the wisdom group (right understanding and right thought). These five factors are simultaneously involved in each moment of awareness and knowing. They are called the working paths (*kāraka magga*). In addition, there are also involved the remaining three factors of the morality group (right speech, right action, and right livelihood), which preserve the precepts through abstention. For example, when the meditator sees or hears any mental or physical object arising, awareness arises with each process without like or dislike and he or she understands the true nature of these processes as impermanent, suffering, and devoid of self. Thus, right understanding and right thought arise in each moment as do right effort, right awareness, and right concentration, upon which right understanding and right thought are dependent. When an intention arises to speak falsely or to commit a wrong action, the meditator is aware of it at that precise moment and so he or she abstains from wrong speech, wrong action, and wrong livelihood. In this way, the meditator applies the Noble Eightfold Path as the preliminary path during vipassanā.

> The view of such a person is the right view; his thoughts are right thoughts; his efforts are right efforts; his mindfulness is right mindfulness; his concentration is right concentration. Even before he starts meditation, the meditator is well established in right speech, right action, and right livelihood. It is in this way that the meditator becomes established in the Noble Eightfold Path.[63]

Knowledge of the Four Noble Truths by Vipassanā

It is only by contemplating the truth of dukkha (the five aggregates) that the Noble Eightfold Path can be developed and the cause of suffering and craving eradicated. Only when the vipassanā path is accomplished can nibbāna be realized. Having seen the true nature of impermanence, suffering, and emptiness in each process, craving for these processes disappears. This is momentary eradication of craving, the truth of the origin of suffering. With cessation of craving, momentary nibbāna, or nirodha, is achieved by means of vipassanā. When comprehension of the Four Noble Truths becomes fully mature, the noble path appears and nibbāna is realized. The preliminary Eightfold Path is transcended and the supramundane state of the noble path is realized. The insight or knowledge developed with vipassanā is discursive knowledge, which has developed by observing sense objects that arise at the sense bases. The insight of the noble path does not have any sense object but is the realization of the Four Noble Truths.

Realization of the Four Noble Truths by the Noble Path

At the culmination of vipassanā insight, the cessation of craving (*nirodha*) is realized. Nibbāna is the cessation of craving, sufferings, and of all things conditioned. Once the meditator has experienced the cessation of dukkha and realized its peace, he or she comprehends that all conditioned states are dukkha. Having recognized them as suffering, there is no longer any craving for them. The origin of suffering (*taṇhā*) is abandoned and the Noble Eightfold Path becomes fully developed.

Vipassanā and the Noble Path

The noble path (*ariya magga*) has been given the full title of "the Noble Truth of the path leading to the cessation of suffering" because it leads to the cessation of all saṅkhāras. But the noble path itself, without the vipassanā path, cannot lead to the attainment of nibbāna where all sufferings cease. In accordance with one's previous perfections (*pāramitā*), one has to practice vipassanā for one's own liberation. The noble path arises as if it had emerged out of the vipassanā path itself. It is for this reason that the vipassanā path is called the preliminary path to the noble path, which is the ultimate goal. The Noble Eightfold Path is a supramundane path, which cannot arise without first following the preliminary vipassanā path. Therefore, the noble path together with the preliminary vipassanā path is called the path leading to the cessation of suffering (*dukkhanirodhagāmini paṭipadā*).[64]

7

Twelve Aspects of Wisdom in the Four Noble Truths

For he who has completed the journey (of existence),
For he who is sorrowless,
For he who is wholly free who from everything,
For he who has destroyed all ties (of fetters),
The fever (of passion) exists not.

Dhammapada, v.90

THERE ARE THREE ASPECTS OF KNOWLEDGE that relate to each of the Four Noble Truths: knowledge of the truth (sacca ñāna), knowledge of the function of the truth (kicca ñāna), and knowledge of the function of the truth that has been performed (kata ñāna). After setting forth the definitions of the Four Noble Truths in the Wheel of Dhamma Discourse, the Blessed One next explained these three aspects of each of the Four Truths. Briefly, these three aspects refer to three aspects or kinds of realization. The first kind of knowledge recognizes that the Noble Truth is indeed true. The second kind of knowledge recognizes what is the appropriate action to take with regard to that particular Noble Truth. And the third kind of knowledge recognizes that the appropriate action has indeed been done with regard to that particular Noble Truth. When one has fully realized all twelve aspects of knowledge with regard to the Four Noble Truths, one has attained enlightenment.

The Truth of Dukkha

> IX. *This is the Noble Truth of suffering. Thus, O bhikkhus, concerning things not heard before, there arose in me the vision, the knowledge, the wisdom, the insight, and the light.*

Knowledge of the Truth (Sacca Ñāna) of Dukkha

Here the Buddha explains how knowledge of the truth of suffering arises. As described previously, all mental and physical phenomena that arise at the sense doors are seen by the noble ones as suffering. In short, the five aggregates of attachment that are regarded as "being" are in fact an ever-changing process, and therefore are dukkha. Life itself is dukkha. The Buddha realized the truth of dukkha through the practice of vipassanā and the attainment of the noble path.

After attaining the arahant path of insight, the Buddha experienced the bliss of nibbāna and understood the five aggregates of attachment as dukkha. This wisdom arose in him not from any teacher, but by direct personal experience after cultivating the Noble Eightfold Path. In the sutta it says, "not heard before." Because the Buddha was a fully self-enlightened one, he is known as a Sammāsambuddha. The extraordinary knowledge which arose in him was described as vision (*cakkhu*), knowledge (*ñāna*), wisdom (*paññā*), insight (*vijjā*), and light (*āloka*). The Buddha used many descriptions so that different audiences could understand his teachings according to their temperaments. In the sense of seeing, knowledge is termed vision; in the sense of knowing, it is called knowledge; in the sense of knowing analytically in several ways, knowledge is termed wisdom; in the sense of knowing penetratively, knowledge is called insight; and in the sense of illuminating (shedding light), it is termed light.

Vision Arose (Cakkhuṃ Udapādi)

The Pāli word *cakkhu* conveys the idea of seeing or vision. The knowledge which sees clearly as if with the physical eye, is termed vision. For example, a man who is blind and suddenly regains his eyesight sees clearly for the first time everything which he had not seen before. Likewise, after one has developed vipassanā insight and path insight, one sees the five aggregates of attachment as dukkha, which before one had not seen clearly because one had been living in delusion. With the development of the noble path insight, a meditator's realization of the true nature of suffering will be even clearer. When it is said, "the vision arose," it is as if there is clear seeing.

Knowledge Arose (Ñānaṃ Udapādi)

The Pāli word *ñāna* signifies knowing or knowledge. It is a common expression of knowing, meaning "ignorance is rooted out."

Wisdom Arose (Paññā Udapādi)

The word *paññā* signifies knowing analytically in various ways. When wisdom arises during vipassanā meditation, the meditator knows the difference between mind and matter, cause and effect, and he or she knows how mental and material processes are arising and passing away every moment. The meditator knows these to be impermanent, suffering, and not subject to anyone's control. Such knowledge is described as knowing analytically. The Buddha, therefore, said that such wisdom had arisen in him.

Insight Arose (Vijjā Udapādi)

Vijjā means penetration, or penetrative insight. Knowing penetratively is derived from the word *paṭiveda*, penetrating through. Just as when hidden by a screen or a wall objects cannot be seen, but when a hole is made in the screen or wall objects become visible through these openings, likewise, this penetrative insight is capable of piercing the veil of delusion, or moha. At first under cover of delusion, what is seen, heard, and so forth is not known as impermanent, suffering, and egoless. Such knowledge is called knowing penetratively. The Buddha, therefore, declared that such penetrative insight had arisen in him.

Light Arose (Aloko Udapādi)

Āloko literally means bright, but is used here to mean illumination or seeing clearly. It refers to the knowledge that discerns all phenomena distinctly. Before path knowledge, the true nature of impermanence, suffering, and selflessness is neither seen nor known. When vipassanā insight and noble path insight are developed, their true nature becomes apparent. The Buddha, therefore, described this light which arose in him.

Knowledge of Function (Kicca Ñāna) of Dukkha

> X. *This is the Noble Truth of suffering which should be fully understood. Thus, O bhikkhus, concerning things not heard before, there arose in me the vision, the knowledge, the wisdom, the insight, and the light.*

When the Buddha says that the Noble Truth of suffering should be understood, he means that one should not run away from life, but should instead strive to understand the suffering of life and investigate it. In vipassanā practice the meditator investigates and observes carefully the five aggregates of attachment in order to understand rightly. The meditator realizes that every process is impermanent because it perishes after arising (*hutvā abhāvato anicca*). Suffering is awesome because it oppresses by incessant arising and passing away (*udayabbaya paṭipilanaṭṭhena dukkhā*) and it is not self or soul because it is not amenable to control. The mind-body process occurs of its own, not subject to one's will (*avasā vattanaṭṭhena anatta*). In this manner, the meditator understands the truth of suffering comprehensively and rightly (*pariññeyya*). While Buddha realized the truth of suffering without having heard it from any one else, disciples can realize the Dhamma only after hearing it from the Buddha or other disciples who have grasped the Dhamma. One should note that the understanding of the truth must come through personal experience, not by hearsay or intellectual understanding.

Knowledge of What Has Been Performed (Kata-Ñāna) with Regard to Dukkha

> *XI. This is the Noble Truth of suffering, which has been understood. Thus, O bhikkhus, concerning things not heard before, there arose in me the vision, the knowledge, the wisdom, the insight, and the light.*

This is how knowledge arose as to what has to be understood with regard to the truth of suffering. The understanding of impermanence, suffering, and no-self at the preliminary stage of vipassanā is not yet a mature understanding. When the meditator observes mental and physical processes, these are understood as impermanent, suffering, and devoid of self, although the true nature of processes which have not been observed may not be understood as such. It is only when vipassanā insight is fully accomplished, and the wisdom of the noble path fully developed, that the cessation of suffering is experienced. Then the truth of suffering is rightly and fully accomplished.

Even at the first stage of wisdom of the noble path, the stream winner (*sotāpatti magga ñāna*) has not yet fully comprehended the truth of suffering. Only when arahantship has been attained is the truth of suffering fully and completely realized. Once the Buddha had gained the arahant path and fruition, and attained full enlightenment, the truth of suffering was fully realized—nothing remained to be done. This realization came through the knowledge of retrospection (*paccavekkhaṇa ñāna*) after attaining the arahant path and fruition.

THE TRUTH OF THE ORIGIN OF DUKKHA

> *XII. This is the Noble Truth of the origin of suffering. Thus, O bhikkhus, concerning things not heard before, there arose in me the vision, the knowledge, the wisdom, the insight, and the light.*

Knowledge of the Truth (Sacca-Ñāna) of the Origin of Dukkha

"This" refers to the three kinds of craving: sensual craving (*kāma-taṇhā*), craving for existence (*bhava-taṇhā*), and craving for annihilation (*vibhava-taṇhā*). These have already been explained. Kāma-taṇhā, sensual craving, is the craving for objects of sensual pleasure that have to be searched and worked for in order to be obtained . It is evident that some people undergo intense suffering, to the extent of losing their lives, while in pursuit of the objects of their desires. Any attempt to curb the craving that has arisen results in suffering and unhappiness. To look and work for things that are not easily attainable is also suffering. The task of protecting or preserving things that are acquired is also very onerous. Whenever one experiences unhappiness or sorrow in life it is mainly due to craving. However, the majority of people are under the delusion that taṇhā is the source of happiness. They consider it blissful to enjoy the pleasures of various sensual objects. If taṇhā is not aroused, in the absence of pleasurable objects, life becomes dull and monotonous. For these individuals, listening to Dhamma is utterly boring while entertainment shows, cinema, TV, and so forth are found to be enjoyable. By nurturing taṇhā one reinforces ignorance latent in the mind.

Pleasurable sights and sounds excite, delight, and produce craving and this craving gives rise to attachment. As a result of attachment, effort has to be put forth for its fulfillment. This produces kamma, or *saṅkhāra*, and sensual craving, or *kāma-bhava*. When the moment of death arises, one of the activities performed in pursuit of craving over a lifetime arises in consciousness as *javana* consciousness, or *abhisaṅkhāra* consciousness. Craving holds onto the mental object which has appeared at the death moment and rebirth consciousness is immediately conditioned upon that death consciousness moment. From the moment of conception in the new life, it may be said that all the sufferings with regard to that new life have begun, having their roots in craving. For the arahant in whom taṇhā has been eradicated, no further rebirth, hence no further suffering, is possible. Therefore, it is evident that sensual desire, kāma-taṇhā, is the real cause of suffering—the truth of the origin of suffering.

Those who aspire to the realms of form and formless spheres and for attainment of jhānic states of absorptions practice tranquillity meditation. They are reborn into the worlds of the form and formless (*rūpa* and *arūpa*) as Brahmās, and they are free from the suffering of physical pains as well as mental afflictions. Their life span is measured in terms of world cycles. From the worldly point of view, their life may be deemed one of happiness, but when their life span is terminated they face death and suffer the agonies of death. They suffer mental distress, too, for not having the wish of immortality fulfilled. After death, troubles and tribulations await them in the sensual sphere (*kāma loka*) to which they are destined. Thus craving for existence (*bhava-taṇhā*) in the Brahmā world is also the truth of suffering. Craving for nonexistence (*vibhava-taṇhā*) after death is also a cause for suffering, since it encourages unwholesome deeds in this life. The nihilist does not fear the repercussions of undertaking unwholesome actions but instead may pursue these unchecked. Having performed unwholesome kamma, nihilists are reborn in the lower realms, and undergo the woes and miseries of those existences. It is certain, therefore, that craving for nonexistence (*vibhava-taṇhā*) arises out of a nihilistic view of life. This is also the truth of the origin of suffering (*samudaya-sacca*).

The Buddha realized these as the root causes of suffering, as he declared, "the vision that arose in me..." Knowing that this is the Noble Truth of the origin of suffering is the knowledge of the truth (*sacca ñāna*). This knowledge arises both before and after the advent of the noble path. At the moment of the path insight, the function of knowing the truth is accomplished, by way of abandoning (*pahāna-paṭiveda*) as well. To summarize: that which knows the Four Truths before, after, and at the moment of path consciousness is the knowledge of the truth (*sacca ñāna*).

Knowledge of Function (Kicca-Ñāna) of the Origin of Dukkha

> *XIII. This is the Noble Truth of the origin of suffering, which should be abandoned. Thus, O bhikkhus, concerning things not heard before, there arose in me the vision, the knowledge, the wisdom, the insight, and the light.*

If freedom from suffering is desired, the root cause of suffering must be removed. For example, in order to cure a disease the root cause of the illness must be eradicated by applying a suitable medicine. In the same way, taṇhā is the root cause of worldly suffering. Because of taṇhā, one has to suffer repeatedly in the rounds of existence (*saṁsāra*). Taṇhā must be uprooted in order to overcome worldly sufferings. Taṇhā is the truth of the origin of suffering which should be given up (*pahātabba-dhamma*).

It is most essential to know how taṇhā is abandoned. The Buddha made the resolution, "Let craving not appear, let it not arise; I shall keep my mind alone by itself, free from craving." Is it possible to maintain such a state of mind? Those believing in the possibility of doing so should actually try to attain this state of mind and see how long they can maintain it. It is impossible to maintain a taṇhā-free mind for a prolonged period of time if craving is not yet totally uprooted. This is because human beings are social beings, living social lives in a sensual realm. One has to suffer the arising of taṇhā because one has not yet subdued it. Therefore, taṇhā needs to be eradicated whenever possible (*pahātabba-dhamma*).

Threefold Taṇhā

There are three kinds of taṇhā which should be eliminated: (1) craving that motivates physical and vocal actions; (2) craving that stimulates the mind in the realm of imagination and fantasy; and (3) craving that is latent in the mind waiting to manifest itself when the situation arises.

Of these, the craving that motivates physical and vocal actions is classified as *vītikkama-kilesa*: those defilements which motivate transgression of ethical conduct. This kind of craving can be eradicated through the application of the moral precepts (*sīla*). For example, the person observing moral precepts does not steal anything belonging to another, even though he or she may desire it; neither does such a person commit sexual misconduct; nor does he or she tell lies; nor take intoxicating substances. In this way craving is kept in abeyance. This is how craving is eliminated by means of sīla, moral precepts.

The craving that arises in the mind due to mental objects (imaginings or fantasies) is defined as *pariyuṭṭhāna kilesa*, and can be eradicated by samādhi, a concentrated mind. For one who practices tranquillity meditation, thoughts, desires, and imaginings about sensuous objects are suspended. Only if the mind is left free to wander on its own is it possible to become lost in thoughts or imagination about desirable sense objects. For those first practicing meditation, and for whom concentration is not yet developed, thoughts of sensuous pleasures arise unabatedly. When concentrative absorption is attained, thoughts regarding gross types of sensual pleasures cease to arise but only for the duration of absorption. This is how samādhi removes the craving for sensuous pleasures by means of suppression (*vikkhaṃbhana pahāna*).

Craving for existence (*bhava-taṇhā*) and craving for nonexistence (*vibhava-taṇhā*) persist even in one who has attained jhānic absorptions. They even remain with some of the brahmās who abide in the realm of jhānic states. Therefore it can be seen that these kinds of craving cannot be eradicated by samādhi or tranquillity meditation. They can only be subdued.

Latent Defilement (Anusaya-Kilesa)

The craving that is latent in the mind waiting to manifest itself when the situation arises is called latent defilements (*anusaya-kilesa*). These defilements are of two kinds: the potential defilements which are latent in the sense objects (*arammaṇānusaya*) and the potential defilements which are latent in the minds of beings (*santanānusaya*). When one perceives some objects at the moment of seeing, hearing, and so on, one is not aware of these as anicca, dukkha, and anatta. Instead, craving for them arises upon thinking of those objects. Such defilements are known as *arammanānusaya.* These kinds of defilements can be dispelled by vipassanā insight. However, vipassanā insight is incapable of removing defilements that may arise in the objects of which one is unaware. The hidden, latent defilements remain unaffected.

The defilement that has not yet been eradicated by the noble path insight, and remains as a latent disposition in the five aggregates of a being, is known as *santanānusaya.* This defilement can only be uprooted by means of the noble path insight which can only be achieved through the culmination of vipassanā insight. Therefore, one should develop vipassanā insight in order to eliminate latent defilements.

The knowledge of function (*kicca-ñāna*) which knows what should be done with respect to the truth of the origin of suffering (*samudaya sacca*) must be developed prior to the advent of the noble path. The knowledge of function(*kicca ñāna*) is advanced knowledge of what should be known, what should be abandoned, what should be realized and what should be developed. To the Buddha, this knowledge appeared without having heard it previously from anyone.

Knowledge of What Has Been Performed (Kata-Ñāna) with Regard to the Truth of the Origin of Dukkha

> *XIV. This is the Noble Truth of the origin of suffering that has been abandoned. Thus, O bhikkhus, concerning things not heard by me before, there arose in me the vision, the knowledge, the wisdom, the insight, and the light.*

The Buddha explained how the knowledge of craving that should be abandoned had been abandoned (*kata ñāna*), through the insight of retrospection. At the first stage of enlightenment, the stage of a stream winner (*sotāpanna*), craving which leads to rebirth in the lower realms of existence is eliminated. At the second stage of enlightenment (*sakadāgāmi*), the grosser forms of craving for sensuous pleasures (*kāma-taṇhā*) are abolished. At the third stage of enlightenment (*anāgāmi*), the subtle forms of craving for sensuous pleasures are eradicated. At the fourth stage of enlightenment (arahant), all kinds of remaining cravings are completely uprooted. Such eradication of craving is referred to as knowing the origin of suffering by the penetrative insight of abandoning (*pahāna-paṭiveda*). The act of abandoning, or eradicating, constitutes knowing what should be known by the noble path. Thus, the truth of the origin of suffering is that which should be abandoned. This abandonment is penetrative abandoning (*pahāna-paṭiveda*).

The knowledge that craving has been eradicated (*kata-ñāna*) is quite important. The goal of practicing vipassanā is to remove defilements together with craving. Attainment of higher insight (the accomplishment of what should be done) is complete only when craving and defilements are eradicated. It is essential to examine oneself to see whether one is really free from craving or not. If craving still remains, then no claim for any attainment of the noble path and fruition is admissible.

THE TRUTH OF THE CESSATION OF DUKKHA

XV. This is the Noble Truth of the cessation of suffering. Thus, O bhikkhus, concerning things not heard before, there arose in me the vision, the knowledge, the wisdom, the insight, and the light.

Knowledge of the Truth (Sacca-Ñāna)

The Noble Truth of the complete cessation of suffering refers to the state of nibbāna that is experienced at the moment of insight into the noble path. When craving is abolished, all sufferings (mind, matter, and conditioning states) cease. Knowing the truth of the cessation of suffering is called *nirodha-sacca-ñāna*. This knowledge arises before and after the noble path insight, and is realized at the moment of the noble path. At the moment of the noble path attainment (*ariya-magga*), the knowledge of truth (*sacca-ñāna*) is the same as the knowledge of the noble path (*ariya-magga ñāna*), which experiences nibbāna by realization.

Knowledge of the Function (Kicca-Ñāna) of the Noble Truth of the Cessation of Dukkha

> *XVI. This is the Noble Truth of the cessation of suffering, which should be realized. Thus, O bhikkhus, concerning things not heard before, there arose in me the vision, the knowledge, the wisdom, the insight, and the light.*

The Buddha said that the truth of the cessation of suffering, nibbāna, should be realized. The knowledge that knows the truth of the cessation of suffering should be realized is called knowledge of the function (*kicca-ñāna*), since it is the knowledge that knows what function is to be performed with respect to the truth of cessation and how realization takes place. At the moment of the full and firm establishment of insight, when there is an equanimity toward all formations (*saṅkharupekkhā-ñāna*) and while observing arising and passing away of phenomena, the pace of awareness accelerates until the objects and awareness (*saṅkhāras*) plunge into a state of cessation where all saṅkhāras come to an end.

At the time of realizing the cessation of all conditioned states, craving also ceases. Thus, cessation of craving is termed the truth of cessation (*nirodha-sacca*), which is known by direct realization of the noble path. Such realization is known as penetrative insight by realization (*sacchikiriya-paṭiveda*). The Buddha accomplished the knowledge of the function of nibbāna through the path and fruition of the final stage of an arahant while sitting at the foot of the Bodhi tree. He continued to recount how he had developed the knowledge of what had been done regarding the truth of cessation.

Knowledge of What Has Been Performed (Kata-Ñāna) with Regard to the Noble Truth of the Cessation of Dukkha

> *XVII. This is the Noble Truth of the cessation of suffering which has been realized. Thus, O bhikkhus, concerning things not heard before, there arose in me the vision, the knowledge, the wisdom, the insight, and the light.*

This is an account of how the knowledge of the Noble Truth of cessation had been realized by means of the attainment of the path and fruition of arahantship. This knowledge arises through the wisdom of retrospection (*paccavekkhaṇa-ñāna*). The meditator who attains absorptions (*jhāna*) and/or the noble path and its fruitions (*magga-phala*) reobserves these after they are achieved.

The Truth of the Path

XVIII. This is the Noble Truth of the path leading to the cessation of suffering. Thus, O bhikkhus, concerning things not heard before, there arose in me the vision, the knowledge, the wisdom, the insight, and the light.

Knowledge of the Truth (Sacca-Ñāna) of the Path

The Noble Truth of the path leading to the cessation of suffering is known in its shortened form as the truth of the path (*magga-sacca*), which is how I will refer to it here. Knowing that the Noble Eightfold Path is the path that leads to the cessation of suffering, nibbāna, it is called the knowledge of the truth (*sacca-ñāna*). This knowledge arises before, after, and at the moment of the noble path. The meditator at first comes to know this by learning or hearsay. It is said that the truth of the path is a Dhamma to be desired, to be aspired for, and to be appreciated. Learning through hearing, the meditator develops a strong intention to practice. Likewise, there should be a strong intention to realize the truth of cessation which a worldling cannot perceive. The realization of the noble path, nibbāna, is not a thing which one can contemplate before attaining. As for the Buddha, just as he experienced the truth of cessation through his own intuitive insight, he also gained the knowledge of the truth of the path through his own intuition. That is why he said, "concerning things not heard by me before." At the moment of the noble path only the cessation of suffering is realized. It is impossible to realize nibbāna without developing the noble path. This is known as penetrative insight by development of the noble path (*bhāvanā-paṭiveda*).

The truth of the path should be developed with direct experience. The noble path cannot develop itself, one must begin by developing the preliminary path (vipassanā) as a first step. For this reason, vipassanā is regarded as the right path that leads to the cessation of suffering (*nirodha*).

Knowledge of Function (Kicca-Ñāna) of the Truth of the Path

XIX. This is the Noble Truth of the path leading to the cessation of suffering which should be developed. Thus, O bhikkhus, concerning things not heard before, there arose in me the vision, the knowledge, the wisdom, the insight, and the light.

Knowing the truth of the path that should be developed within oneself is called the knowledge of function (*kicca-ñāna*). It is the knowledge that knows what should be developed. One should remember that the truth of dukkha should be fully understood with direct experience and the truth of the path should be developed within oneself. The aim of the development of the path is to experience the bliss of nibbāna, and the practice of vipassanā meditation is essential practice for the development of the noble path. The truth of suffering can be realized through the preliminary path of vipassanā. During vipassanā meditation the meditator observes mental and material aggregates, which appear at every moment. The meditator develops first the insight of distinction between the object and its awareness. This is followed by understanding the cause and its effect. As the meditator proceeds, he or she comes to know the nature of perpetual change or flux. The phenomenal world is constantly arising and passing away. It is impermanent, suffering, and devoid of self. The personal realization of these realities is right understanding (*sammā-dṭṭthi*). When right understanding is developed, right thought (*sammā-saṅkappa*) and other paths have also been developed. When the path of vipassanā is developed and becomes fully established, the Noble Eightfold Path has also evolved.

Intellectual understanding of the phenomena of aggregates is good as a foundation prior to the advent of the noble path. But it should be remembered that knowing the function of the noble path is *kicca-ñāna*, which should be developed through vipassanā and the noble path. In this way, one realizes the truth of cessation, or nibbāna.

Knowledge of What Has Been Performed (Kata-Ñāna) with Regard to the Noble Truth of the Path

> XX. *This is the Noble Truth of the path leading to the cessation of suffering, which has been developed. Thus, O bhikkhus, concerning things not heard before, there arose in me the vision, the knowledge, the wisdom, the insight, and the light.*

When reobserving with the wisdom of retrospection (*paccavekkhaṇa-ñāna*), the Buddha realized that the Noble Eightfold Path had been fully developed at the attainment of the path of arahantship. The three aspects of knowledge—realization (*sacca*), function (*kicca*), and accomplishment (*kata*)—with respect to the Four Noble Truths have now been explained in twelve ways, that is, in terms of the fourfold three aspects of knowledge.

These are summarized below.

1. Knowing the four truths before, after, and at the moment of the arising of the path is called *sacca-ñāna*, or knowledge of the truth. This knowledge consists of knowing: (1) this is the truth of suffering; (2) this is the truth of the origin of suffering; (3) this is the truth of the cessation of suffering; and (4) this is the path leading to the cessation of suffering.

This knowledge arises in advance of the path. For disciples, the knowledge of the truth of cessation and the path is acquired before the arising of path consciousness (path insight) by only hearsay or learning (*sutamaya-ñāna*). The truth of cessation experienced at the moment of the arising of path insight, in addition to the remaining three truths, is also accomplished at the moment of path insight as complete understanding (*pariññā*), abandoning (*pahāna*), and developing (*bhāvanā*).

2. Prior knowledge of what should be known, what should be abandoned, what should be realized, and what should be developed is *kicca-ñāna*, or the knowledge of function. Knowledge of the function consists of knowing: (1) that dukkha should be fully understood; (2) that the origin of suffering (*samudaya*) should be abandoned; (3) that the cessation of suffering (*nirodha*) should be realized; and (4) that the path leading to the cessation of suffering should be developed. This knowledge arises before vipassanā meditation starts, as well as during vipassanā practice, but prior to the advent of the noble path.

3. Knowing that what should be done has been done is called *kata-ñāna*. If the four functions of fully understanding, abandoning, realizing, and developing have been accomplished, this fact is known through the wisdom of retrospection. This is known as the knowledge of completion of what has to be done.

These are the twelve kinds of knowledge that are made up of the four truths: the fourfold knowledge of realization; the fourfold knowledge of function; and the fourfold knowledge of what has been done. Of these twelve, it is important to know clearly how the knowledge of truth arises and how the four functions are to be performed. A brief description follows:

1. The Noble Truth of dukkha should be fully comprehended; such comprehension is known as *pariññā-paṭiveda.*
2. The Noble Truth of the origin of dukkha should be abandoned; such abandonment is known as *pahāna-paṭiveda.*

3. The Noble Truth of cessation should be realized; such realization is known as *sacchikiriya-paṭiveda.*
4. The Noble Truth of the Path should be developed; such development is known as *bhāvanā-paṭiveda.*

It should be noted that when the meditator realizes cessation, nibbāna, at the arising of path insight, all four truths are simultaneously accomplished.

VIPASSANĀ AND THE FOUR NOBLE TRUTHS

During vipassanā practice, the Four Noble Truths are accomplished temporarily. If the meditator observes the physical and mental processes of the five aggregates as meditation objects (realizing them to be impermanent, suffering, and devoid of self) this is considered understanding the truth of suffering. At that moment, craving cannot arise; this is the temporary abandonment of craving (*tadaṅga-pahāna-paṭiveda*). At the same time, the delusion (*avijjā*) that would misapprehend the observed object as permanent, happiness, and self, temporarily ceases. Consequently, when delusion ceases, other conditional formations (*saṅkhāras*) that arise when conditioned by delusion also cease. This is realization through temporary cessation (*tadaṅga-nirodha*). The vipassanā path is developed every moment through understanding the true nature of anicca, dukkha, and anatta. This is *bhāvanā paṭiveda.* While practicing vipassanā meditation by knowing the truth of dukkha through awareness, the remaining three truths are accomplished by the completion of the tasks of abandoning (*pahāna*), realizing (*sacchikiriya*), and developing (*bhāvanā-paṭiveda*). Thus, all four truths are developed during vipassanā practice.

> *XXI. As long, O bhikkhus, as my vision of true knowledge was not fully clear in these three aspects and in these twelve ways regarding the Four Noble Truths, I did not claim to have realized the perfect enlightenment that is supreme in the world with its devas, māras, and brahmās, in this world with its recluses and brāhmaṇas, with its princes and men.*

The Buddha's attainment of the insight of the arahant path is called *sammā-saṃbodhi,* fully self-enlightened, because insight was achieved without instruction from others (*sammā + saṃ + bodhi*: *sammā*, rightly or fully; *saṃ*, oneself; *bodhi*, knowledge). Through this wisdom the Buddha knew rightly and perfectly everything that was to be known. Therefore, it is also called *sabbaññuta-ñāna*, to know everything. *Pacceka-buddhas* (silent buddhas) are also self-enlightened (*sambuddha*), but are unable to teach the Dhamma to others. Their enlightenment is not as full as the sammā-saṃ-buddhas. If the disciple (*sāvaka*) attains the insight of the arahant path it is simply known as bodhi, knowledge or enlightenment, without any attributions, such as, *sammā* (rightly) or *saṃ* (oneself).

When the Buddha attained the state of enlightenment, the knowledge that knows all Dhammas (*sabbaññuta-ñāna*) also arose simultaneously. After acquiring this faculty of knowing everything, buddhahood was attained. Therefore, the full self-enlightenment (*sammā-saṃbodhi*) is regarded as the knowledge responsible for the attainment of buddhahood. According to the above passage, the Buddha said he had not yet declared the attainment of perfect enlightenment which gives rise to buddhahood.

For how long did he withhold this admission of buddhahood? It was stated that he withheld it for as long as his knowledge of the Four Noble Truths in the three aspects and twelve ways was not fully clear to him. There were some recluses and leaders of religious sects at the time of the Buddha who claimed themselves to be enlightened, to know everything of the past, present, and the future. When learned people, recluses, and laymen began to scrutinize them, they were found to fall far short of their claims. The Buddha, therefore, reiterated that he had not previously claimed omniscience (*sabbaññuta*) before his attainment of full self-enlightenment (*sammā-saṃbodhi*).

THE BUDDHA'S ENLIGHTENMENT

XXII. But when, O bhikkhus, my vision of true knowledge was fully clear in these three aspects and in these twelve ways regarding the Four Noble Truths, then I claimed to have realized the perfect enlightenment that is supreme in the world with its devas, māras, and brahmās, in this world with its recluses and brāhmaṇas, with its princes and men.

After the knowledge of seeing reality as it is (*yathābhūta-ñāna*), fully clear in the three aspects and twelve ways, the Buddha declared his attainment and realization of the incomparable, the most excellent and perfect enlightenment, the perfectly enlightened supreme buddhahood. This declaration was made not just to that region, to that part of the world, but to the whole universe with its powerful devas of sharp intellect, with its māras hostile to the true teaching, and with its more powerful and highly intelligent brahmās. It also included the whole of the human world with its learned recluses and brāhmaṇas, with its kings and many peoples.

This declaration was an open invitation to all to investigate the Buddha's claim and to have their inquiries answered by him. This is, indeed, a very bold, solemn declaration that was not made impulsively without due reflection, but made only after the Buddha had reassured himself by the wisdom of retrospection that he had really attained buddhahood.

> *XXIII. Indeed, a vision of true knowledge arose in me thus: My mind's deliverance is unassailable. This is the last birth. Now there is no more becoming.*

In this passage, the Buddha states that the deliverance of his mind was unshakable. This is to distinguish between the ultimate deliverance of nibbāna and deliverance that is the result of the attainment of meditative absorptions. For those who achieve absorption concentrations or jhānic states, the mind is free from defilements, such as, sensual desire and ill will. These defilements remain calm, suppressed in the mind. But when their absorptions deteriorate, sensual desire, ill will, and so forth arise again. These jhānic states only suppress the defilements for a period of time (*vikkhambhana*). The deliverance won by the Buddha was obtained through complete eradication of the defilements (*samuccheda-pahāna*), including traces of defilements (*paṭipassaddhi vimutti*). Deliverance is achieved by complete eradication of the defilements and is the result of the path and fruition of arahantship. These deliverances remain steadfast and unshakable. Therefore, the Buddha reflected, "the deliverance of my mind is unshakable."

As explained previously, the main cause of rebirth, or continuity of existence, is craving, taṇhā. When the Buddha attained arahantship, craving was totally uprooted. Therefore, he said that there would be no more rebirth or becoming for him. The Buddha reflected soon after his enlightenment under the Bodhi tree:

> Through many a birth I wandered in saṁsāra,
> Seeking, but not finding, the builder of the house.
> Sorrowful is it to be born again and again.
> O house-builder (craving)! Thou art seen.
> Thou shalt build no house again.
> All thy rafters are broken. Thy ridgepole is shattered.[65]

Buddhas and arahants who have eradicated craving completely must still live life like others since their present existence has been brought forth by craving before craving had become eradicated. Therefore it is said, "This is the last birth. Now there is no more becoming (rebirth)." These are the concluding words of the Blessed One.

Through greed, hatred, and delusion, overwhelmed by greed, hatred, and delusion, one aims at one's own ruin, at others' ruin, at the ruin of both, and one suffers mental pain and grief. If, however, greed, hatred, and delusion are given up, one aims neither at one's own ruin, nor at others' ruin, nor at the ruin of both and one suffers no further mental pain and grief.

> Thus is nibbāna realizable even during this lifetime, immediate, inviting, attractive, and comprehensible to the wise. Now, insofar as the bhikkhu has realized the complete extinction of greed, hatred, and delusion, insofar is nibbāna realizable, immediate, inviting, attractive, and comprehensible to the wise.
>
> *Anguttara Nikāya, 1.158*

REFLECTIONS AND ACCLAMATIONS ON THE DHAMMA

XXIV. Thus the Buddha spoke. The group of five bhikkhus wasglad and acclaimed his words. While this doctrine was being expounded, there arose in the Venerable Kondañña the pure, immaculate vision of the truth and he realized, "Whatsoever is subject to causation is also subject to cessation."

These words of rejoicing were recorded by the reciters at the First Council, which was held immediately after the Buddha's passing away into nibbāna. This was in order to show how the group of five bhikkhus were gladdened by the discourse. The record states that the Venerable Kondañña became a stream winner during or at the end of the sermon. For the Venerable Kondañña, indeed, during the hearing of the sermon, the progress of insight became developed with each moment. He came to know the Four Noble Truths as they should be known, and attained the path and fruition of the stream winner while listening to the discourse. The knowledge of Kondañña is considered stainless because when he attained the state of the stream winner his mind became free from lust (*rāga*), free from defilements of wrong view (*diṭṭhi*), and free from doubt (*vicikicchā*). When one attains the state of the stream winner, the mind becomes free from defilements and the eye of wisdom is opened. One sees or realizes nibbāna at that very moment.

When did the eye of wisdom open? At the moment when Kondañña realized that everything that has the nature of arising also has the nature of dissolution. There are two modes of realization at this stage. Realizing by means of vipassanā insight is the moment of developing insight into the arising and passing away of phenomena. Vipassanā insight is fully developed at the stage of equanimity of formations, while observing the continuous process of the arising and dissolution of phenomena (mind and body), a stage is reached at which all formations cease completely and the peace of nibbāna is experienced. This is realization by means of the noble path of insight.

> *XXV. When the Buddha expounded the discourse, thus putting into motion the turning of the wheel of Dhamma, the devas of the earth exclaimed: "This excellent wheel of Dhamma which could not be expounded by any ascetic, brāhmaṇa, deva, māra, or brahmā in this world, has been put into motion by the Blessed One at Deer Park, in Isipatana, near Varanasi.*
>
> *Hearing this, the devas Catumahārājika, Tavatiṃsā, Yāmā, Tussitā, Nimmānarati, Paranimmitavasavati, and the Brahmās Brahmāpārisajjā, Brahmāpurohitā, Mahābrahmā, Parittābhā, Appamāṇabhā, Ābhassarā, Parittasubhā, Appamāṇasubhā, Subhakiṇṇā, Vehapphalā, Avihā, Atappā, Sudassā, Sudassī, and Akaniṭṭhā also raised the same joyous cry.*
>
> *Thus, at that very moment, at that very instant, this joyous cry extended as far as the brahmā realm. These ten thousand world systems quaked, tottered, and trembled violently. A radiant light, surpassing the radiance of the devas, appeared in the world.*

When the Buddha set in motion the wheel of Dhamma, the earth-bound devas proclaimed in one voice: "The incomparable wheel of Dhamma has been set in motion by the Blessed One in Isipatana, at the Sage's Resort, near Varanasi, a motion which no recluse nor brahman nor any deva nor mara nor brahmā nor any other being in this world can reverse."

Having heard this proclamation by the earth-bound devas, catumahārājika devas, the devas in the upper realms, and the brahmās all proclaimed in unison. In a single instant, the voice of proclamation went forth up to ten thousand universes. The entire cosmos of myriad world systems shook upwards and downwards, and trembled in all four directions. An immeasurable sublime radiance, caused by the mighty and profound teaching, surpassed even the majestic divine radiance of the devas appearing on earth.

> *XXVI. Then the Buddha said, "Friends, Kondañña has indeed understood. Friends, Kondañña has indeed understood." Therefore, the Venerable Kondañña was named Aññāsi Kondañña—"Kondañña who understands."*

At the end of the discourse, the Buddha perceived that Kondañña had attained the knowledge of the stream winner. Therefore, he made this utterance: "Friends, Kondañña has indeed understood. Friends, Kondañña has indeed understood." It was in reference to this utterance that Kondañña became known as "Aññāsi Kondañña."

The Venerable Kondañña who, having seen the truth (*diṭṭha-dhammo*), arrived at the truth (*patta-dhammo*), clearly knew (*vidita-dhammo*) and penetrated the truth (*pariyogāḷa-dhamma*); who, having overcome doubt (*tiṇṇavicikiccho*) and become free from skepticism (*vigatakathaṃkatho*), having acquired courage of conviction in the teaching (*vesārajjapatto*) and become independent of others (*aparapaccayo*) in the dispensation of the Buddha, requested in these words: "Lord, may I have leave to take up the ascetic life, in the presence of the Buddha. May I receive the higher ordination."

The Buddha permitted him to join the order with these words: "O bhikkhu, come (*ehi bhikkhu*)." He then said, "Well taught is the Dhamma. Come and practice the holy life for the sake of the complete ending of suffering." Kondañña was already an ascetic, but not of the Buddha's order. He, therefore, asked for admission. When the Buddha said, "Ehi bhikkhu," he acknowledged Kondañña's entry into the order.

There was a group of only five monks from the human world who heard the first sermon, but the *Milinda Pañhā*[66] states that 118 million brahmās and innumerable devas attained to the higher knowledge upon listening to the Buddha's discourse. Among the five monks, only Kondañña attained to higher knowledge. The remaining four: Vappa, Bhaddiya, Mahānāma, and Assaji, had not yet attained to higher knowledge. After Kondañña was admitted to the order, the Buddha gave guidance and instructions on the practice of the Dhamma to the remaining four members of the group. Then Vappa and Bhaddiya attained the higher knowledge. The Buddha accepted their request for admission into the order by saying, "*Etha bhikkhu*" (Come bhikkhus). The Buddha then gave instructions to Mahānāma and Assaji without going on the alms-rounds for food for himself. Three bhikkhus are said to have gone out for alms food and all the six, including the Buddha, sustained themselves on the food brought back by the other three. Being thus guided and instructed by the Buddha, the stainless eye of wisdom arose in Mahānāma and Assaji. Having seen, having reached, having clearly understood, and having penetrated through to the Dhamma, leaving uncertainty behind, having overcome all doubts, being free from wavering resolution, having acquired the courage of conviction with respect to the teaching, having personal knowledge of the Dhamma, not depending on others with regard to the teaching, they made this request to the Buddha:

> May we, Lord, have leave to take up the ascetic life, in the presence of the Buddha; may we receive higher ordination in the order.

The Buddha replied:

> *Etha bhikkhu*, come bhikkhus, well taught is the Dhamma. Come and practice the holy life for the sake of the complete ending of suffering.[67]

This invitation by the Buddha is the act of ordination and, accordingly, Mahānāma and Assaji became bhikkhus in the order of the Buddha's dispensation. According to the Pāli Vinaya text,[68] the four ascetics attained the higher knowledge in two groups of two each, whereas the commentaries stated that they attained the higher knowledge one by one as follows:

Kondañña attained the higher knowledge on the full-moon day of July, the same day the Buddha taught the sermon. Vappa, Bhaddiya, Mahānāma, and Assaji attained the higher knowledge on the first, second, third, and fourth waning days respectively. And on the fifth day, the Buddha assembled all five bhikkhus together and taught them the *Discourse on the Characteristics of Non-self* (*Anattalakkhaṇa Sutta*). At the end of this discourse, all five bhikkhus attained arahantship, the final stage of sainthood. There were then six arahants, including the Buddha in the world—a truly wonderful event.

May all beings be happy and experience the bliss of nibbāna!

Notes

1. Anguttara Nikāya 1.145; Gradual Sayings 1.128
2. The Buddha's Ancient Path 12.13
3. Majjhima Nikāya 1.163, 1.164
4. Majjhima Nikāya 1.240
5. Majjhima Nikāya 1.167
6. Majjhima Nikāya 1.241, 1.244
7. Majjhima Nikāya 1.245, 1.246
8. Saṁyutta Nikāya 2.28; Anguttara Nikāya 1. 50
9. Majjhima Nikāya 1.249
10. Majjhima Nikāya 1.249
11. Majjhima Nikāya 1.250
12. Majjhima Nikāya 1.167
13. Vinaya Piṭaka 1.1-10
14. Majjhima Nikāya 1. 171
15. Dīgha Nikāya 1.40
16. Dhammapada Verse 277,278, 279
17. Saṁyutta Nikāya 3.138
18. Dhammapada Verse 160-165
19. Dhammapada Verse 276
20. Majjhima Nikāya 1.371
21. Vinaya Piṭaka 1.233; Anguttara Nikāya 4.179
22. Dhammapada Verse 185
23. Dhammapada Verse 146
24. In the original discourse of the *Dhammacakkappavattana Sutta*, which appeared in the Vinaya Piṭaka, the words "sickness is suffering" (*byādhi*

pi dukkho) is found in the list of sufferings, but the passage "sorrow, lamentations, pain, grief, and despair are suffering" (*soka-parideva-dukkha-domanassu-pāyāsā pi dukkhā*) is missing. However, in other suttas and in the Abhidhamma, the word "sickness, byādhi" is not found in the list, while the passage, "sorrow, lamentations, pain, grief, and despair" is included. The commentaries, including *Visuddhimagga*, did not mention sickness (*byādhi*) in the definition of the Truth of Suffering. These different readings were cited in the sub-commentary of the Vinaya Piṭaka (*Sāratthadīpanī*). The sub-commentary was written in Sri Lanka during the reign of King Parakkamabāhu (1153–1186 C.E.). The great commentators, Buddhaghosa, Dhammapāla, etc. who wrote exegeses on the *Dhammacakkappavattana Sutta* in the Pāli canon, did not mention the different readings in the suttas. Buddhaghosa and Dhammapāla lived between the fifth and eighth centuries C.E. They were silent on this point because at that time there were no differences in the readings of the Vinaya Piṭaka, Sutta Piṭaka, or Abhidhamma Piṭaka. Therefore, the word sickness (*byādhi*) should be replaced by "sorrow, lamentation, pain, grief, and despair" (*soka-parideva-dukkha-domanass-upāyāsa*), which themselves encompass sickness.

25. Vinaya Piṭaka 1.9
26. Vinaya Piṭaka 1.10
27. Dīgha Nikāya 1.36
28. Saṁyutta Nikāya 2.28; Anguttara Nikāya 1.50
29. Majjhima Nikāya 2.312
30. Anguttara Nikāya 1.190–192
31. Dīgha Nikāya 2.312
32. Dīgha Nikāya 2.312
33. Dīgha Nikāya 2.312
34. Dīgha Nikāya 2.312
35. Dīgha Nikāya 2.312
36. According to the commentary, the *Visuddhimagga*, vipassanā (bare insight meditation) produces a one-pointedness of mind and a capacity to overcome hindrances that is akin to the access concentration experienced in the jhānic states (absorbed concentrations). However, it is

emphasized that this one-pointedness of mind is in no way similar to absorption concentration (appanā samādhi) and therefore, is only figuratively called access concentration. A more accurate rendering of this term would be vipassanā samādhi, insight concentration or khanika samādhi, momentary concentration.

37. Dīgha Nikāya 2.312
38. Anguttara Nikāya 3.284
39. Dīgha Nikāya 2.312
40. Anguttara Nikāya 3.415
41. Saṃyutta Nikāya 5.143
42. Anguttara Nikāya 4.422
43. Dīgha Nikāya 1.387
44. Dīgha Nikāya 2.312
45. Saṃyutta Nikāya 1.62
46. Saṃyutta Nikāya 1.40
47. Saṃyutta Nikāya. 5.421; SN. 3.158
48. Saṃyutta Nikāya 2.22
49. Anguttara Nikāya 3.415
50. Majjhima Nikāya 3.218
51. Anguttara Nikāya Aṭṭhakathā 78
52. Saṃyutta Nikāya 5.437
53. The Path of Purification 699
54. Majjhima Nikāya 1.294
55. Anguttara Nikāya 1. 223
56. Dhammapada Verse 216
57. Saṃyutta Nikāya 4.251
58. Udāna Pāli 80
59. Saṃyutta Nikāya 3.151
60 Saṁyutta Nikāya 5.431; Dīgha Nikāya 2.90; Vinaya Piṭaka 1.231

61. The Path of Purification 700
62. Paṭisaṃbhidāmagga 2.62
63. Majjhima Nikāya 3.289
64. Esa lokuttaro ariyo aṭṭhaṅgiko maggo, saha lokiyena maggena dukkhanirodhagāminipaṭipadāti saṅkhaṁ gato.—Vibhaṅga Aṭṭhakathā 114
65. Dhammapada Verse 153, 154
66. Milinda Pañhā P. 331
67. Vinaya Piṭaka. 1.13
68. Vinaya Piṭaka 1.12, 13

Glossary

All words are from the Pāli language, unless otherwise indicated.

abhijjhā: covetousness

abhiññā: higher knowledge, supernormal knowledge

abhisamaya: the moment of awakening, enlightenment

abhisaṅkhāra: volitional formation, new conditioning

abyāpāda: without ill will

acetana: static

adhicitta: higher consciousness

adhimokkha: determination

adhimutti: resolution

adhisīla: higher morality

ādīnava: danger; misery

adosa: non-hate

ājīva: livelihood

ājīvaka: naked ascetic

ājīvapārisuddhi sīla: morality of pure livelihood

akiriyavāda: doctrine of non-action

akusala: unwholesome

āloka: light, illumination

amata: deathlessness, nibbāna

anāgāmi: never returner, non-returner (third stage of realization)

ānāpāna: in- and out-breath, inhalation and exhalation

ānāpānasati: mindfulness of the in-breath and the out-breath

anatta: non-self

anekantavāda: doctrine of many possibilities

anicca: impermanent

aññathābhāva: radical change

aññoñavāda: doctrine of one the other

anusaya: underlying, latent disposition or tendency

anupādisesa: (nibbāna) without the substratum (aggregate) remaining

āpo: water

āpo dhātu: element of water, the quality of cohesion in material form

appanā: absorption concentration

arahant: the perfected one who has eliminated all passions

arahatta: the quality of being an arahant, arahantship

ariya: noble, noble one

ariyamaggañāna: insight of the noble path

arūpa: formless, the realm of formless brahmas

asammoha: nonconfusion, non-delusion

asaṅkhata: unconditioned state, nibbāna

āsava: taint

āsavakkhayañāna: knowledge of the destruction of the taints *ātman (Skt.):* soul, self

attabhāva: person, personality, self-hood, rebirth

attan, atta: soul, self

attavāda: doctrine of self

avihiṃsā saṅkappa: thoughts free from cruelty

avijjā: ignorance

avijjāsava: taints of ignorance

avikkhepa: non-distraction

āvuso: friend

avyakta (Skt.): things that are not manifest

bahujana: many people

bhaṅga: dissolution

bhava: becoming

bhava taṇhā: attachment for becoming or life

bhāvanā: development, meditation

bhavaṅga: life continuum consciousness

bhavāsava: taints of becoming

bhāvetabba: to be developed

bhaya: fear

bhikkhu: an almsman, a monk

bhūmi: ground, soil, place; stage, realm

bhūmikkama: (order of teaching the Noble Eightfold Path) according to realms

bīja: seed

bodhi: enlightenment, awakening

bodhimaṇḍala: vicinity of the Bodhi tree where the Buddha achieved enlightenment

bodhisatta: the aspirant for enlightenment, the future Buddha

bojjhaṅga: enlightenment factor

brahman: absolute reality, suchness in Hinduism

brahmā: sublime being

brahmaṇa: sacred books of Hinduism, Brahmanism

brahmavihāra: divine abiding

buddhi: enlightenment

byādhi: sickness

cāga: generosity

cakkhu: eye

cakkhu-viññāṇa: eye consciousness

catuyāma: four precepts

cetanā: volition

cetasika: mental state, concomitant

chanda: will, zeal

citta visuddhi: purity of mind

cuti: death

dāna: giving, generosity

desanā: teaching

desanākkama: (order of teaching the Noble Eightfold Path) according to the teaching

deva: celestial being, "god"

Dhamma: the law or teaching of the Buddha

dhamma: state, thing, phenomenon, mental object

dhātu: element

diṭṭha: sees, knows

diṭṭhi: view, belief

diṭṭhi visuddhi: purity of view

domanassa: grief

dosa: hate, ill will, anger

duggati: unhappy destination, unhappy rebirth

dukkha: suffering

dvāra: door

ekaggatā: one-pointedness of mind

gati: destination, destiny, place of rebirth

ghana: compact

ghāna: nose

gocara: *resort, domain*

gotrabhū: the insight that enters another lineage

guṇa: special quality and modes, the primary constituents of nature in Sāṃkhya philosophy

hadaya: heart

hadaya vatthu: heart basis (physical basis of the mind)

iddhi: power, success

indriyasaṃvara sīla: the morality of restraining the senses

iriyāpatha: posture

Isipatana: the sage's resort

jāti: birth, caste

javana: speed, impulsion (consciousness)

jhāna: meditative absorption

jhānalābhī: one who accomplishes absorption

kāma: sensuality

kāmacchanda: lust or zeal for sense pleasures

kāmāsava: taints of the sense pleasures

kāma-loka: sensual plane

kāma-rāga: greed for sense pleasures

kamma: action, deed

kamma bhava: becoming, present action

kamma-niyāma: the law of kamma

kammapatha: course of action

karma (Skt.): action, deed

kāraka: doer

karunā: compassion

Kāsi: ancient province of Varanasi

kāya: body; group

khandha: aggregate, group

khañika: momentary

khantī: patience

khema: security

khetta: field

kicca: function

kilesa: defilement

kiriyā: functioning

koṭṭhāsa: part

kṣatriya (Skt.; Pāli. khattiya): warrior caste

kusala: wholesome, skillfulness

lobha: greed

loka: the world or universe, life

lokiya: mundane, worldly

lokuttara: supramundane

magga: path, path insight

maggadātā: one who shows the way

mahābhūta: primary material element

mahaggata: exalted

mana: mind

māna: conceit, pride

manasikāra: making mind, attention

mantra: chants, hymns

māra: obstructors and evil beings

maraṇa: death, dying

māyā: illusion, ignorance

mettā: loving-kindness

mettā bhāvanā: development of loving-kindness

micchā: wrong

moha: delusion, ignorance

mohakkhayo: extinction of delusion

mokkhadātā: one who gives salvation

mudu: tender

mūla: basic

muñcitukamyatā: desire for deliverance

nāma-rūpa: mind-and-matter; mentality-and-materiality

ñāna: knowledge, insight, realization

ñāta: knowing

ñānadassana: insight and vision

nandī: delight

nekkhamma-saṅkappa: thoughts free from sensual desire, renunciation

nibbāna: nibbāna, extinction (of greed, hate, and delusion)

nibbidā: disgust

nicca: permanent

nimitta: sign

nirodha: cessation (of dukkha)

nīvaraṇa: hindrance

niyāma: cosmic law

niyatavāda: doctrine of fate or destiny, fatalism, determinism

obhāsa: illumination

ogha: flood

paccavekkhaṇā: reobservation

paccayapariggaha: insight that distinguishes between cause and effect

paccayasannissita sīla: the morality of the proper use of requisites

pacceka: private, by oneself

padhāna: basic, principal; endeavor, effort

pahāna: abandonment, eradication

pahānakkama: (teaching of the Noble Eightfold Path) according to the order of eradicating

pahātabba: to be uprooted

pañcakkhandha: five aggregates

pañcasīla: the five basic precepts of morality for Buddhist laymen and laywomen

paññā: wisdom

paṇidhi: desire, aspiration

paṇīta: sublime

papañca: obstacle, diversification

parama sukha: excellent, happiness

paramattha: highest sense, ultimate

pāramitā: perfection

parideva: lamentation

parikamma: preliminary

parinibbāna: complete extinction of aggregates, final liberation

pariññā: profound knowledge

pariññātabba: to be fully understood

pariyogāḷa: penetrates

pariyuṭṭhāna: obsession

pasanna: gladdened

passaddhi: tranquility

pathavī: earth

pathavī-dhātu: the element of earth, the quality of heaviness and lightness in material form

paṭibhāganimitta: counterpart sign

paṭicca: having depended, due to, dependent on

paṭiccasamuppāda: dependent origination, causal genesis

paṭigha: resentment

paṭimokkhasaṃvara sīla: the morality of the vows of the monastic order

paṭipadā: way, practice, path

paṭipassaddhi: calmed

paṭipattikkama: process of practice, the order in practice

paṭiveda: penetration

patta: arrives

phala: fruition

phassa: contact

pīti: rapture, joy

prakṛti (Skt. Pāli. pakati): nature, material form

pubbabhāga: preliminary

puggala: person

purisuttama: man par excellence, superman

purusa: God in Vedas, essence or subject in Sāmkhya philosophy

puthujjana: ordinary man, worldly man

rāga: attachment

rajas (Skt.): light, passion

rūpa: form, matter

rūpakkhandha: form or matter aggregate

sabbaññuta: omniscient knowledge

sabhāva: individual essence

sacca: truth, reality

sacchikātabba: to be realized

sacetana: dynamic

saddhā: confidence, faith, devotion

sakadāgāmī: once returner (second stage of realization)

sakkāya diṭṭhi: the concept of self

saḷāyatana: sixfold base

samaṇa: sage, recluse

samāpatti: attainment

samatha: serenity

samatha bhāvanā: development of concentration

sammā: right

sammā ājīva: right livelihood

sammā diṭṭhi: right understanding

sammā kammanta: right action

sammā saṅkappa: right thought

sammā samādhi: right concentration

sammā sati: right mindfulness

sammā vācā: right speech

sammā vāyāma: right effort

sammasana: grasping, comprehending, thorough knowing

sammuti: convention

sammuti sacca: conventional reality

sampajañña: comprehension, full awareness

saṁsāra: wheel of life, round of rebirth, transmigration

samuccheda: cutting off

samudaya: the origin or the cause (of suffering)

saṃvara: restraint

saṁyojana: fetter

sangha: the order, community

saṅkhāra: formation, conditions, action and reaction

saṅkhārupekkhā: equanimity of formations

Sāṇkhya: rationalism, one of six systems of Indian philosophy

saññā: perception, recognition

santati: continuity

santi: peace

sāsana: dispensation

sassata-diṭṭhi: the view of eternalism

sat (Skt.): existence

sati: mindfulness

satimā: mindful

satta: a being

sattva (Skt.): goodness

saupādisesa: with the substratum (aggregate) remaining

sekha: trainer

sikkhāpada: training precept

sīla: morality, moral discipline

sīla visuddhi: purity of morality

śudra (Pāli. sudda): servant, the lowest caste in Hindu society

somanassa: joy, mental pleasure

sotāpanna: one who enters the stream of noble path, stream winner, stream enterer (first stage of realization)

suddhi: purity

sukha: happiness

sukkha vipassaka: bare insight

sutta (Skt. sūtra): discourse of the Buddha

Sutta Piṭaka: the "basket" or collection of the Buddha's discourses

tadaṅga: temporarily

tamas (Skt.): dullness, darkness (in Sāṇkhya philosophy)

taṇhā: thirst, craving, desire

taṇhākkhayo: destruction of craving

tapas (Skt.): heat energy

Tathāgata: the Buddha, perfect one

tathatā: true nature, suchness

tejo: fire

tejo-dhātu: fire element, the quality of heat and cold in material form

thina-middha: stiffness and torpor

tiṇṇavicikicchā: overcomes doubt

tiraṅa: overcome, investigate

uccheda-diṭṭhi: the view of nihilism

uccheda-vāda: the doctrine of nihilism

udagga: exultant

udayabbaya: rising and passing away

upacāra: access, neighborhood

upādāna: attachment

upādāya: derivative or secondary (materiality)

upakkilesa: imperfection

upāsaka: a lay follower of the Buddhadhamma

upasama: peace (term for nibbāna)

upasamānussati: contemplation on peace or the quality of nibbāna *upāsikā*: a female lay follower of the Buddhadhamma

upāyāsa: despair

upekkhā: equanimity

uppāda: arising

uppattikkama: (the Noble Eightfold Path) according to the order of arising

vācā: speech

vaiśya (Skt.; Pāli. vassa): cultivator, trader

vāyāma: effort

vāyo: air

vāyo-dhātu: the element of air, the quality of motions in the material form

Veda: the collection of hymns, the sacred book of Hinduism

vedanā: feeling

vesārajjapatto: acquires courage of conviction in teachings

vibhava: non-being, non-becoming

vibhava-taṇhā: attachment for nonexistence

vicikicchā: doubt

vidita: having known

vigatakathaṅkatho: overcomes skepticism

vihiṁsā: cruelty

vijjā: insight, knowledge, clear vision

vikappa: alternative

vikkhambhana: dispelling, put away, suppression

vimokkha: liberation

vimutti: release

vinaya: monastic discipline

viññāṇa: consciousness, mind

vipāka: resultant, fruition

vipallāsa: hallucination

vipariṇāma: subsequent change

vipassanā: insight, wisdom

vipassanāyānika: one whose vehicle is insight

vipaṭipatti: wrong theory

virāga: devoid of lust

viriya: energy, effort

visuddhi: purification

vitakka: applied thought

vitha: street, thought process

vītikkama: transgression

viveka: seclusion

vuṭṭhānagāminī-vipassanā: insight leading to emergence (of the path)

vyakta (Skt.): things that are manifest

yathābhūta: as it is

BIBLIOGRAPHY

Pāli Texts

Aṅgutta-aṭṭhakathā. Chaṭṭhasaṅgāyanā edition. Rangoon, Burma (Myanmar), 1970.

Anguttara Nikāya. Edited by Rev. Richard Morris. London: Pali Text Society, 1885.

Dhamma. Varanasi, India: Sanskrit University, 1972.

Dhammapada-aṭṭhakathā, Chaṭṭhasaṅgāyanā edition, Rangoon, Burma (Myanmar), 1969.

Dīgha Nikāya. Edited by J.E.Carpenter. London: Pali Text Society, 1912–17.

Itivuttaka. Edited by Ernst Windisch. London: Pali Text Society, 1889.

Kathāvatthu Muḷaṭīkā. Chaṭṭhasaṅgāyanā edition. Rangoon, Burma (Myanmar), 1960.

Majjhima Nikāya. Edited by V. Trenckner. London: Pali Text Society, 1888.

Milinda Panhā. Chaṭṭhasaṅgāyanā edition. Rangoon, Burma (Myanmar), 1982.

Paṭisambhidāmagga. Edited by Arnold C. Taylor. London: Pali Text Society, 1905–07.

Saṁyutta Nikāya. Edited M. Leonfeer. London: Pali Text Society, 1880–98.

Suttanipāta. Edited by V. Fausboll. London: Pali Text Society, 1885.

Theragāthā and Therigātha. Edited by H. Oldenberg and R. Pischel. London: Pali Text Society, 1883.

Udāna. Edited by P. Steinthal. London: Pali Text Society, 1885.

Vinaya Piṭaka (Vinaya Mahāvagga). Edited by Hermann Oldenberg. London: Pali Text Society, 1879.

Vibhṅga-aṭṭhakathā. Chaṭṭhasaṅgāyanā edition. Rangoon, Burma (Myanmar), 1968.

Visuddhimagga and Its Commentary (Devanāgarī). Edited by Dr. Rewata Dhamma. Varanasi, India: Sanskrit University, 1972.

TRANSLATIONS

Bhikkhu Bodhi. *The Discourse on the All Embracing Net of Views.* Kandy, Sri Lanka: Buddhist Publication Society, 1978.

Bhikkhu Ñāṇamoli. *The Path of Purification.* Kandy, Sri Lanka: Buddhist Publication Society, 1975.

Bhikkhu Ñāṇamoli and Bhikkhu Bodhi. *The Middle Length Discourses of the Buddha: A New Translation of the Majjhima Nikāya.* Boston: Wisdom Publications, 1995.

Mahāsī Sayādaw. *The Great Discourse on the Wheel of Dhamm.* Translated by U Ko Lay. Rangoon, Burma: Buddhasāsanuggaha Organization, 1981.

Walshe, Maurice. *The Long Discourses of the Buddha: A New Translation of the Dīgha Nikāya.* Boston: Wisdom Publications, 1995.

GENERAL BOOKS

Ambedkar, Dr. B.R. *The Buddha and His Dhamma.* Bombay: Siddharth Publications, 1974.

Nārada Mahāthera. *The Buddha and His Teachings.* Malaysia: Buddhist Missionary Society, 1973.

Nyanaponika Mahāthera. *The Heart of Buddhist Meditation.* London: Rider Pocket Edition, 1983.

———. *Path to Deliverance.* 4th ed. Kandy, Sri Lanka: Buddhist Publication Society, 1982.

Piyadassī Mahāthera, *The Buddha's Ancient Path.* Kandy, Sri Lanka: Buddhist Publication Society, 1974.

Rāhula Mahāthera, Walpola. *What the Buddha Taught.* London: Gordon Fraser, 1978.

Radhakrishnan, S. *A Sourcebook in Indian Philosophy.* 12th ed. Princeton: Princeton University Press, 1989.

Sīlānanda, Ven. U. *The Four Foundations of Mindfulness.* Boston: Wisdom Publications, 1990.

Wisdom Publications

Wisdom Publications is a not-for-profit publisher dedicated to making available authentic Buddhist works for the benefit of all. We publish translations of the sutras and tantras, commentaries and teachings of past and contemporary Buddhist masters, and original works by the world's leading Buddhist scholars. We publish our titles with the appreciation of Buddhism as a living philosophy and with the special commitment to preserve and transmit important works from all the major Buddhist traditions.

If you would like more information or a copy of our mail order catalog, and to keep informed about our future publications, please write or call us at:

Wisdom Publications
199 Elm Street
Somerville, Massachusetts 02144, USA
Telephone: (617) 776-7416 • Fax: (617) 776-7841
Email: info@wisdompubs.org • www.wisdompubs.org

The Wisdom Trust

As a not-for-profit publisher, Wisdom Publications is dedicated to the publication of fine Dharma books for the benefit of all sentient beings and dependent upon the kindness and generosity of sponsors in order to do so. If you would like to make a contribution to Wisdom, you may send it to our Somerville office. If you would like to sponsor the publication of a book, please write or email us for more information.

Thank you.

Wisdom Publications is a non-profit, charitable 501(c)(3) organization and a part of the Foundation for the Preservation of the Mahayana Tradition (FPMT)